Insurance
Solvency
Supervision

ORGANISATION FOR ECONOMIC CO-OPERATION AND DEVELOPMENT

ORGANISATION FOR ECONOMIC CO-OPERATION AND DEVELOPMENT

Pursuant to Article 1 of the Convention signed in Paris on 14th December 1960, and which came into force on 30th September 1961, the Organisation for Economic Co-operation and Development (OECD) shall promote policies designed:

— to achieve the highest sustainable economic growth and employment and a rising standard of living in Member countries, while maintaining financial stability, and thus to contribute to the development of the world economy;
— to contribute to sound economic expansion in Member as well as non-member countries in the process of economic development; and
— to contribute to the expansion of world trade on a multilateral, non-discriminatory basis in accordance with international obligations.

The original Member countries of the OECD are Austria, Belgium, Canada, Denmark, France, Germany, Greece, Iceland, Ireland, Italy, Luxembourg, the Netherlands, Norway, Portugal, Spain, Sweden, Switzerland, Turkey, the United Kingdom and the United States. The following countries became Members subsequently through accession at the dates indicated hereafter: Japan (28th April 1964), Finland (28th January 1969), Australia (7th June 1971), New Zealand (29th May 1973) and Mexico (18th May 1994). The Commission of the European Communities takes part in the work of the OECD (Article 13 of the OECD Convention).

Publié en français sous le titre :

LE CONTRÔLE DE LA SOLVABILITÉ DE L'ASSURANCE

FOREWORD

The insurance sector has recently undergone a number of internal and external developments. This has resulted, in some cases, in inadequacy of tariffs, technical provisions, equity capital or investments and has led to insolvency situations.

These factors, together with the greater role insurance companies currently play in national economies (for example, in the fields of life inssurance and pensions, or as institutional investors), have led governments to strenghten their monitoring of this important financial sector.

With a view to meeting Member countries' growing concern over these developments, in early 1993 the OECD's Insurance Committee decided to create a Group of Governmental Experts on Insurance Solvency. According to its mandate, this Group's primary task is to survey and analyse the regulatory and supervisory systems and techniques existing in Member countries concerning the solvency of insurance companies, the main issues currently raised in this field and measures and practices used or that could be used to address them.

As a basis for their work, the experts of each of the Member countries initially drafted a summary report on the supervision of solvency in their country. The experts were asked to cover the following points in their presentations:

– regulations concerning the supervision of solvency;
– practical organisation of supervision;
– recovery measures when difficulties arise.

These national reports have been brought together in this publication. It provides an overview of regulations and practices for the supervision of insurance companies *before* difficulties arise, and designed primarily to prevent the latter from occurring, which remains the primary goal of governments. It also describes measures that can be taken *after* difficulties arise, either to prevent them from worsening or to deal with them, or, failing that, to organise the liquidation of the company in the best interests of society at large.

These national contributions constitute an unique single reference document, which the Insurance Committee approved for publication at its 54th Session in December 1994.

The information in this work is up-to-date as at 1 December 1994. This publication was prepared by the Directorate for Financial, Fiscal and Enterprise Affairs, and is published on the responsibility of the Secretary-General of the OECD.

TABLE OF CONTENTS

AUSTRALIA

The Insurance and Superannuation Commission (ISC) was established in 1987 to integrate into a single office the Government's supervisory and policy roles in the areas of insurance and superannuation. The ISC supervises approximately 160 authorised general insurers and 50 registered life insurance companies. The major pieces of legislation for ensuring the financial soundness of companies carrying on life and general (non-life) insurance business in Australia are the *Life Insurance Act 1945* and the *Insurance Act 1973*, respectively. In addition, under the *Insurance Acquisitions and Take-overs Act 1991*, the Treasurer can prohibit proposed acquisitions of insurance companies, if the proposals are considered to be contrary to the public interest.

Government regulation of the life and general insurance industry aims to protect the interests of policyholders and the viability of the financial sector to promote confidence in the industry. Regulation is not aimed at controlling the daily market operations of companies, but provides and enforces prudential guidelines within which the industry can safely operate. The role of the ISC is not, however, to guarantee the interests of policy-holders and shareholders against loss in the event of company failure.

I. Regulations concerning the supervision of solvency

A. *Life insurance*

The *Life Insurance Act* sets out the following capital and solvency requirements for registered life insurance companies:

- companies incorporated in Australia are required at all times to have minimum paid-up share capital of at least $A 10 million;
- companies without share capital (mutual companies) are required at all times to maintain $A 10 million in eligible assets (other than the assets in a statutory fund);
- foreign companies are required at all times to maintain in Australia $A 10 million in eligible assets (other than assets in a statutory fund); and
- all companies registered under the Act are required to maintain an excess of eligible non-statutory fund assets over non-statutory fund liabilities of not less than $A 5 million.

"Eligible assets" excludes certain assets invested in related companies.

"Statutory funds" are established within life insurance companies to receive premiums, hold assets and pay policy obligations and other expenses in relation to life insurance business of the relevant fund. Other than as prescribed under the *Life Insurance Act,* assets of a fund must be used only with respect to policies written into that fund and not for any purpose associated with policies written under another fund. The assets of each statutory fund must be kept distinct from all other assets of a company. As such, any income earned by fund assets must be reinvested in the fund by which it was earned.

The policy liabilities attributable to each statutory fund must be actuarially determined each year and each fund must have assets sufficient to cover these policy liabilities as well as any other liabilities of the fund (*e.g.* taxation, creditors). For traditional forms of life insurance, the actuarial assessment of policy liabilities must be at least as great as that base on the conservative basis laid down in the *Life Insurance Act* (*i.e.* a net premium basis with conservative interest and mortality bases). For newer, unbundled investment products if short term investment guarantees are provided, the liability must include the account balance payable to policyholders plus a mismatching reserve to cover market risk if assets other than short term fixed interest assets are used to back such business.

In July 1993, the Australian Government announced that it would introduce a new regulatory regime for the life insurance industry.

A major change under the new regime will be the treatment of solvency. As noted above, solvency is currently assessed on the basis of a company maintaining the required excess, as prescribed in legislation, of eligible assets over liabilities. As the solvency of statutory funds is a critical indicator of a life company's capacity to meet policy obligations, it is proposed that solvency standards apply to individual statutory funds, based on an actuarial analysis of a fund's assets and liabilities. As a consequence, a solvency standard will be established for each statutory fund having regard to the unique size and structure of that fund's future obligations.

A fund will satisfy the proposed solvency standard if it is in a financial position to meet all existing liabilities and where and adequate allowance is made for future expected income from premiums and earnings from assets and expected future outlays on claim payments and other expenses. Failure of any statutory fund of a life company to meet this standard would allow the ISC to intervene in a company's operations and could lead to the appointment of a judicial manager.

Also under the proposed amendments, a new "capital adequacy standard" will be introduced. This is the amount that would be necessary for a company to continue normal operations as a going concern. The amount required for capital adequacy will be greater than that required for solvency. To satisfy this requirement, a company must be able not only to meet existing liabilities but also ensure that the liabilities arising from future new business will be met as they fall due. Failure of any statutory fund of a life company to meet this standard would result in closer scrutiny by the ISC.

Rather than prescribing a "capital adequacy standard", individual companies will be required to maintain a financial position whereby additional assets are held above the solvency standard in accordance with Professional Actuarial Standards. Actual amounts for a given company depend on its individual method of operation and future business plans.

The "margin on services" method of actuarial valuation of liabilities will be adopted as the standard method of valuation for determining the policy liabilities of statutory funds. This method is based on gross premiums and provides for future profit margins to be identified, spread over the life of the policy and gradually released as the policy ages. Earnings will also be generated as the actual experience varies from the expected. The assumptions about future experience that are to be used at each yearly valuation are best estimate assumptions and so will change from year to year. In the new financial statements the policy liabilities will therefore be a realistic of best estimate amount which will enable the profit of a statutory fund to be determined realistically. The balance sheet will show the best estimate policy liabilities and specific solvency reserves which a company needs to meet the solvency standard. Assets above the solvency standard will reflect the fund's and the company's overall strength.

B. General insurance

The *Insurance Act 1973* ensures that authorised general insurance companies can cover claims liabilities if and when they occur, and increases confidence of insureds, and the public generally, that claims will be met. Authorised insurers are required to have paid-up share capital of not less than $A 2 million.

The Act also requires an insurer authorised to conduct insurance business in Australia to meet the following solvency requirements on an ongoing basis:

– for companies incorporated in Australia, assets must exceed liabilities by not less than $A 2 million, 20 per cent of premium income, or 15 per cent of outstanding claims, whichever is the greater;
– for all companies, including overseas companies operating in Australia through branches, assets in Australia must exceed Australian liabilities by not less than $A 2 million, 20 per cent of premium income, or 15 per cent of outstanding claims, whichever is the greater.

Authorised insurers should maintain a reasonable margin over and above the minimum solvency requirements to cover such events as fluctuations in market values of assets. They are also required to comply with guidelines which ensure that risk and event retention levels are at a prudent level when compared to available capital.

A company's solvency margin is determined on a net account basis (*i.e.* net of reinsurance). Consequently, the company's reinsurance arrangements are required to be approved.

Assets must be held in the name of the insurer and in custody subject to its control. Therefore, while it is permitted to use in-house or external fund managers to professionally manage an insurer's assets, direct legal ownership must remain with the insurer. Several classes of investments are specifically excluded from the solvency calculation (or are subject to approval). In particular, most investments in related companies (where there is a more than 25 per cent interest) are subject to approval.

Lloyd's underwriters fall within the jurisdiction of the *Insurance Act,* but are subject to different conditions than those applying to authorised insurers. They must lodge with the Treasurer Government securities with a market value of not less than $500 000. They must also lodge a covenant by an Australian bank for an amount equal to the total of Lloyd's underwriter's premium income in Australia in the preceding calendar year. These two requirements represent funds that are available to satisfy claims in Australia by a policyholder against Lloyd's.

II. The practical organisation of this supervision

A. *Life insurance*

The ISC has a comprehensive program in place to ensure that life companies comply with the provisions of the *Life Insurance Act.* Companies are required to submit financial data on a quarterly and annual basis regarding the full range of their financial activities. The ISC supplements its analysis of this data with an ongoing program of "on-site" inspections. Through these inspections, the ISC develops an understanding of each company's business plans, organisational arrangements, quality of management, systems capabilities and internal controls.

In addition to the supervisory function performed by the ISC, the Act vests responsibility for the determination of solvency margins in the "appointed actuary". The appointed actuary is required by law to provide the ISC with an annual assessment of the financial condition of a company, a statement on the valuation of the company's liabilities and the actuarial reserves included in those estimates of liability. The appointed actuary may be either an employee of, or a consulting actuary to, the life office.

Under proposed amendments to the *Life Insurance Act,* the supervisory powers of the ISC will be strengthened. The ISC will have specific powers to seek information, investigate life companies and to issue enforceable "directions" to companies regarding solvency standards and capital adequacies.

New financial statements will report life company solvency and earnings in a way that improves comparability and accountability. Life companies will be required to provide annually to the ISC a profit and loss statement and a balance sheet, the detail of which is to be determined by the ISC. This is intended to allow the flexibility to respond to market developments.

The enhanced role of auditors and appointed actuaries gives them rights and responsibilities including a duty to report to the ISC. To facilitate this, they have qualified privilege. The appointed actuary must produce a confidential annual report on the financial condition of the company, and this report must comment on the degree to which the company complies with the capital adequacy standard.

B. *General insurance*

The ISC's approach to the administration of the *Insurance Act* is one of supervision rather than regulation.

There are a number of statutory and administrative procedures to ensure the ISC can properly assess the financial soundness of insurers. These measurers are largely historical in nature, *e.g.* returns are submitted after a balance date, and reflect management decisions taken well before that date. In order to consider the future viability of an insurer, the ISC consults regularly with each company and with the industry broadly on areas of interest. In doing so, it develops an understanding of a company's business plan, quality of management and systems capabilities. Regular contact with industry associations ensure the ISC is aware of issues and developments impacting on the industry as a whole.

As a general example of these requirements, companies are required to:

- have an approved auditor;
- on request, obtain an actuarial assessment of their liabilities;
- inform the ISC within 21 days of any changes of key particulars related to their authorisation; and
- lodge audited annual returns, within four months of the end of the financial year.

An authorised insurer is required to comply with prescribed minimum financial standards and is subject to continuous supervision. An authorised insurer who fails to comply with the required standards, or appears to be in danger of falling below the standards, can be subject to investigation. Following any such investigation, directions may be issued to the company as to the future conduct of its business.

III. Measures when difficulties arise

A. *Life insurance*

A range of powers are available to the ISC under the *Life Insurance Act* to protect the interests of policyholders. Generally, these powers include:

- requiring the production of books and access to premises for the purpose of determining whether a life company has complied or is complying with provisions of the Act;
- directing the company not dispose of, or otherwise deal in a specified asset(s) where it appears a life company is, or is likely to become, unable to meet its liabilities; and
- appointing an inspector to make an investigation of the whole or part of the business of the company where a life company is, or is likely to become, unable to meet its obligations.

If, following an investigation, the ISC considers it appropriate, it can approach the Court to order that the company be placed under judicial management or wound-up. A Judicial Manager has responsibility for reporting to the court on courses of action that are in the best interests of owners and policyholders. These can include:

- the transfer of the business to another company;
- the carrying on of the business of the company; or
- winding-up the company.

B. General insurance

The *Insurance Act* provides significant powers of investigation and direction where it appears a company may be unable to meet its liabilities. These include:

- requiring an authorised insurer to appoint an independent actuary to report on its liabilities;
- appointing an inspector to examine and report on the company's affairs, including whether the company should be wound up;
- issuing directions to the insurer, including directions to freeze assets and cease issuing new policies; and
- applying to the Court to have a company's operations wound-up.

Any person or company conducting insurance business without authorisation is liable to a fine of $2 000 per day in the case of a person or $20 000 per day in the case of a company.

The Act contains secrecy provisions. These provide for the confidentiality of information relating to individual companies and are an important support in obtaining adequate information about early changes in an insurer's operations.

AUSTRIA

Introduction

The tasks of the Austrian Supervisory Authority are based on the Insurance Supervisory Act (VAG 1978), which has undergone a large number of amendments, most recently amendments in 1994 containing the adoption to the third generation of EC directives (life and non-life).

I. Regulations concerning the supervision of solvency

The basic objective of supervision of insurance companies in Austria is to ensure adequate protection for policyholders and beneficiaries. There are many rules aiming at supervising the companies' economic situation. One basic requirement is the company's obligation to possess a minimum solvency margin, which is one measurement of financial health of an insurance company.

A. Solvency requirement

The Austrian regulations on solvency supervision follow the EC Directives. In principle the solvency requirement depends on the company's business volume (*i.e.* variable solvency requirement). But in any case a minimum solvency margin – expressed in terms of absolute figures – is required in order to ensure that undertakings possess adequate resources when they are set up and that in the subsequent course of business the solvency margin shall not fall below a minimum amount.

1. Variable solvency requirement

Taking into account the mathematical reserves and the capital at risk (life insurance) and the yearly premium income and average amount of claims incurred (general insurance business) the solvency requirement varies with the course of business. A deduction of ceded reinsurance up to a certain percentage is allowed.

a) Non-life insurance

The Austrian calculation rules for *non-life insurers* which are based on the Article 16 of the First Non-life Insurance Directive (73/239/EEC) can be summarized as follows:

The solvency requirement to be constituted is determined either by the premium index or the claims index.

• Premium index

The written premiums of the last financial year are divided into 2 portions (below and over 10 million ECU). 18 per cent of the first portion and 16 per cent of the second portion are calculated and then added. The result is multiplied by the ratio existing in respect of the last financial year between the amount of claims for own account and the gross amount of claims. The percentage applied must not however be lower than 50 per cent.

• Claims index

For the calculation of the claims index the average of claims over the last three financial years (in some cases seven years) are divided into two portions (the triggering amount is seven million ECU). 26 per cent of the first portion and 23 per cent of the second portion are calculated and then added. The result is multiplied by the ratio existing in respect of the last financial year between the amount of claims for own account and gross amount of claims (a minimum of 50 per cent is required).

The amount of the solvency margin must be at least equal to the higher of these two indices, but in no event should be less than the minimum solvency requirement (as described under 2 below).

In case *health insurance* is practised on a similar technical basis to that of life insurance the solvency requirement is reduced to a third.

b) Life insurance

The Austrian calculation rules for life assurers follow Article 19 of the First Life Insurance Directive (79/267/EEC).

The solvency requirement is calculated as follows: 4 per cent of the mathematical reserves (a deduction of ceded reinsurance up to 15 per cent is possible) and 0.3 per cent (for certain cases 0.1 per cent or 0.15 per cent) of the capital at risk (a deduction of ceded reinsurance up to 50 per cent is possible) are calculated and then added. The solvency margin must be at least equal to this sum, but in no case fall below the minimum solvency requirement.

In certain cases the percentage for calculating the capital at risk is lower: for *temporary assurance* on death of a maximum term of three years it is 0.1 per cent. In case the term is between three and five years it is 0.15 per cent.

For *unit-linked business* the calculation is equal to that of life insurance. In case the insurance undertaking doesn't bear any investment risk, the term of the contract exceeds five years and the allocation to the cover management expenses set out in the contract is fixed for a period exceeding five years 0.1 per cent of the mathematical reserves has to be calculated. If the company doesn't cover a death risk, the capital at risk is not included into the calculation.

2. *Minimum solvency requirement*

The Austrian Insurance Supervisory Act requires a minimum solvency margin. As to undertakings transacting only life insurance (sickness insurance; other non-life insurance) it is 50 (30; 30) million Sch. In case the undertaking is active in more than one class it is for life insurance: 40 million Sch for sickness insurance: 20 million Sch and for other non-life insurance: 20 million Sch. For foreign insurers the amounts are halved.

B. *Elements which constitute the solvency margin*

The solvency margin correspondents to the assets of the company free of any foreseeable liabilities. The following elements are taken into account to constitute the solvency margin:

a) paid up share capital and half of the unpaid share capital,
b) reserves,
c) carry forward profits,
d) subordinated capital subject to some limitations,
e) profit reserves, if they may be used to cover losses, and
f) bidden reserves up to 20 per cent of the sum of funds as described under *a)* and *b)*.

Upon calculation of the solvency margin the following elements have to be deducted:

a) loss of the financial year,
b) own shares,
c) securities concerning own subordinated capital,
d) intangible assets.

II. Practical organisation of the solvency supervision

A. *General*

The supervision of insurance companies is carried out by the Austrian Insurance Supervisory Authority which is part of the Ministry of Finance. It is entitled to intervene in any matter of insurance undertakings' activities as far as the interests of the insured persons are concerned and to issue provisions which are necessary to protect these interests.

Information on the financial situation of insurance companies is mainly obtained from financial returns of the undertakings which are sent to the Insurance Supervisory Authority. Once a year (no later than 6 months after the end of the financial year concerned) the insurance companies have to forward to the Supervisory Authority their duly approved and audited financial annual accounts (together with the annual reports) including a confirmation of the insurance company's solvency status. In case of life insurance, sickness insurance and other non-life insurance (as far as the two latter are operated on a technical basis similar to that of life insurance) an actuary has to certify that the technical provisions are calculated on an actuarial basis and are in conformity with the relevant legal provisions.

The insurance companies have to complete forms, giving more detailed information about the structure of the items of the balance sheet and the profit and loss account. Quarterly the undertakings have to forward a list of assets, covering mathematical reserves. All this information is processed via EDP. It is the basis for further investigations by the authority, which is authorized to carry out on-the-spot investigations of insurance companies.

Generally speaking the Austrian Insurance Supervisory Authority monitors the financial health of the insurance undertakings, including the solvency status of the company, the establishment of sufficient technical provisions and the covering of those provisions by matching assets.

B. *Solvency supervision*

Solvency supervision of an insurance company starts with granting a licence, then it is carried out regularly, at least on an annual base. Supervision of solvency ends with the winding-up of a company.

The Austrian Supervisory Authority, organized in 4 departments, checks if insurance undertakings asking for a licence possess adequate financial resources. At least once a year it controls if the undertakings meet the solvency requirements, in order to be permanently capable to meet the obligations arising from the insurance contracts. The Supervisory Authority analyses the returns of the insurance companies, verifies the datas directly with the undertakings, carries out regular on-the-spot investigations and looks at the current financial development of the companies.

III. Measures when difficulties arise (recovery measures)

In case the company's own funds fall below the solvency requirement the undertaking has to submit a plan for the restoration of a sound financial position for approval to the Supervisory Authority *(solvency plan).*

The guarantee fund is usually one third of the solvency requirement, but must not be less than 50 (30; 30) million S as to undertakings transacting only life assurance (sickness insurance; accident insurance) and 40 (20; 20) million S as to undertakings transacting life assurance (sickness insurance; accident insurance) and being active in more than one branch. (The amounts are halved for foreign insurance companies). In case the company's own funds fall below the guarantee fund, the undertaking has to submit a short term financing scheme for approval to the Supervisory Authority *(finance plan).*

The Supervisory Authority is authorized to *prohibit free disposal* of all or part of the assets of the insurance company, if:

- the company's own funds fall below the solvency requirements and a deterioration of the financial situation is expected;
- the company's own funds fall below the guarantee fund; or
- if the company hasn't established sufficient technical provisions or if the technical provisions aren't covered by matching assets.

The Supervisory Authority is authorized to *withdraw the licence* if the insurance company fails to take measures to fulfil the solvency (or the finance) plan within the prescribed time.

BELGIUM

I.   Regulations concerning the supervision of solvency

The solvency of insurance companies is supervised in a number of areas.

A.   *Solvency margins*

The regulations on supervision follow the EC Directives regarding the solvency margin that an insurance company should have in both life and non-life business in order to cover operating risks.

The solvency margin constituted corresponds to the assets of the company, free of any foreseeable liabilities, less non-disposable intangible items.

1.   The following elements are taken into account to constitute the solvency margin relating to non-life and life business:

- the paid-up authorised capital plus paid-in surplus or, for a mutual insurance association, the initial paid-in funds plus members' accounts that satisfy certain criteria;
- half of the unpaid authorised capital of the company or the initial funds, provided that at least 25 per cent of the total capital or of the initial funds is paid up;
- uncommitted reserves, whether statutory or free;
- profit or loss brought forward from previous years;
- subordinated debt, subject to the following limitations:
  - Aggregate subordinated debt may constitute no more than 50 per cent of the margin, and fixed-term subordinated debt no more than 25 per cent.
  - For an issue to be taken into account, the indenture must stipulate that, in the event of the insurance company's bankruptcy or liquidation, the debt shall be subordinate to all other claims and shall be redeemable only after all other outstanding liabilities have been settled.

Furthermore, subordinated debt is taken into account only in respect of the proceeds actually received, and provided that the issue complies with regulations.

- perpetual securities and other instruments; (Only the proceeds actually received shall be taken into account, and the total of such securities plus the subordinated debt referred to above shall not together constitute more than 50 per cent of the margin. To be taken into account, the debt must also satisfy the following conditions:
  - It is not redeemable without the prior approval of the Office of Insurance Supervision.
  - The indenture gives the insurance company the option to defer interest payments.
  - The lender's claims on the insurance company are entirely subordinate to those of all unsubordinated creditors.
  - The documents regulating the issue of the securities stipulate that losses may be offset by the debt and unpaid interest without preventing the insurance company from continuing its business.)

2. *The following elements are taken into account to constitute the solvency margin relating to non-life business only:*

   - the amount of supplementary contributions for which a mutual association may assess its members for the year, up to one-half the difference between the maximum supplementary contribution that may be assessed under the by-laws, and contributions already notified, with this amount not exceeding 50 per cent of the margin;
   - on application by the company, with supporting documents, to the Office of Insurance Supervision, capital appreciation due to undervaluation of assets, provided that this capital appreciation is not exceptional.

3. *The following elements are taken into account, on application by the company, with supporting documents, to constitute the solvency margin relating to life business only:*

   - capital appreciation due to undervaluation of assets or overvaluation of liabilities other than life insurance provisions, provided that this capital appreciation is not exceptional;
   - a percentage of future life insurance profits of the company, within the limits set by regulations;
   - the undepreciated acquisition costs contained in the technical provisions, within the limits set by regulations.

The amount of the *solvency margin to be constituted* for non-life insurance is determined in relation to either annual premiums or the average of claims over the last three financial years (sometimes seven years).

For life insurance, a different basis is used, which is based on the amount of mathematical provisions and the level of risk-reserve capital.

The regulations require a minimum solvency margin (or a minimum guarantee fund) of an amount which varies for different insurance branches and fluctuates in line with the European currency unit, subject to a threshold, however, for non-life insurance.

B. Technical provisions

Insurance companies are required to calculate and enter in their accounts under the heading of technical provisions their commitments under the insurance contracts they have issued and for the purpose of complying with the relevant laws and regulations. These technical provisions must be constituted on a gross basis (including reinsurance).

Insurance companies must set aside sufficient technical provisions and book sufficient technical liabilities to be able at all times to meet all their commitments under insurance contracts.

1. *Technical provisions for non-life insurance* must comprise:

   – A provision for unearned premiums and outstanding risks.
   The provision for unearned premiums corresponds to the portion of gross premiums (including reinsurance) that must be allocated to the following financial year, or to later years, to cover claims, administrative costs and investment management expenses.
   The provision for outstanding risks is supplementary to the provision for unearned premiums. It is constituted if it is estimated that the total of claims and administrative costs arising from outstanding policies and yet to be incurred by the company will exceed aggregate unearned premiums and premiums payable under the said policies.
   – A provision for claims.
   This provision corresponds to the estimated ultimate total cost to the company of all claims to date, whether reported or not, less any amounts already paid out in respect of those claims. It includes indemnities and internal and external claims management costs.
   No deduction may be made to allow for interest income on investments, except as permitted by the Office. Unrealised recoveries, including accidental damage excess to be recovered, may not be deducted from the provision for claims.
   – A provision for equalisation and catastrophe risks.
   This provision is constituted in order to compensate for a non-recurring technical loss, to smooth out fluctuations in the claims rate, or to cover special risks, in the years ahead.
   It must be set up for the following risks: credit risk, risks due to natural elements, risks in the area of nuclear power, liability risks arising from pollution or defective products, aerospace risks and risks of terrorism and labour conflict.
   – A provision for ageing.
   Where rates increase with age, this provision corresponds to the estimated present value of the insurance company's future commitments, less the estimated present value of future premiums.

- A provision for distribution of profits, including premium refunds allocated but not yet paid out.
- Any other provision the Office might require.

2. *Technical provisions for life insurance* must comprise:

- A provision for life insurance.
  This provision is calculated in accordance with the regulations governing life insurance.
- A provision for claims.
  This provision corresponds to benefits accrued but not yet paid, and to the corresponding external and internal management costs.
- A provision for distribution of profits, including premium refunds allocated but not yet paid out.

C. Assets representing technical provisions

Technical provisions and liabilities must at all times be backed up by equivalent assets that belong in full to the insurance company and are set aside to guarantee its commitments towards policyholders and beneficiaries, by separate branch (life, non-life).

1. *Assets representing technical provisions and liabilities must take into account the type of business carried out by the insurance company in order to ensure the safety, profitability and liquidity of its investments; the insurance company must ensure that its investments are sufficiently diversified and dispersed. In addition, the assets representing provisions must be located:*

- In the European Community, in the case of Belgian companies. Financial assets located outside the EC are also acceptable, provided that the National Bank, or a credit establishment licensed by the Banking and Finance Commission or by the competent authority of an EC Member country in which that credit establishment is headquartered, certify that it holds those assets, on the insurance company's behalf, through an EC establishment, in a financial institution established outside the EC and licensed by a public body which is located in a Member country of the OECD and which performs a role similar to that of the Banking and Finance Commission.
- In Belgium, for Belgian establishments of third-country enterprises. Financial assets located outside Belgium are also acceptable, provided that the National Bank, or a credit establishment that is licensed or whose establishment has been registered by the Banking and Finance Commission, certify that it holds those assets, on the insurance company's behalf, through an establishment in Belgium, in a financial institution established outside Belgium and licensed by a public body which is located in a Member country of the OECD and which performs a role similar to that of the Banking and Finance Commission.

The location of an asset, real or financial, signifies the presence of that asset within the borders of a given country. Assets in the form of financial claims are considered to be located in the country in which they may be redeemed.

Assets representing provisions must satisfy regulatory matching requirements.

2. *In addition, such assets must belong to one of the following categories of investments:*

   - bonds;
   - equities and other variable-income securities;
   - shares in collective investment undertakings that invest in cash, other financial assets and real estate;
   - other money and capital market instruments;
   - call or put options on financial assets, futures contracts, and other derivative instruments that are traded on a regulated market that is liquid, recognised and open to the public, and that function in a normal manner by helping to reduce investment risk or by enabling the portfolio to be managed efficiently;
   - loans backed by sufficient guarantees;
   - real estate, claims thereon or real estate certificates;
   - claims on reinsurers (such claims need not be located in the EC, but they must be acknowledged in writing by the reinsurers and collateralised, under terms acceptable to the Office);
   - reinsurers' share in technical provisions, under terms acceptable to the Office;
   - claims on insurance buyers and intermediaries, arising from direct insurance transactions, except for claims in respect of premium payments that are more than one month overdue;
   - claims arising from recovery or subrogation and relating to branch 14 transactions (although such claims may be designated in respect of this separate branch only);
   - uncontested tax claims;
   - demand deposits or term deposits at the National Bank or a credit establishment licensed by the Banking and Finance Commission or by the competent authority of an EC Member country in which that credit establishment is headquartered;
   - policy loans, if authorised under the regulations governing the life insurance business (although such loans may be designated only in respect of the separate "life" branch referred to in Section 9);
   - interest and rent accrued but not yet due on the designated assets (although such interest and rent may be designated only in respect of the same separate branch as the corresponding assets; furthermore, interest accrued but not yet due may be designated only if it is not already included in the value of an asset belonging to another category);
   - the Office may, under exceptional circumstances and for the duration thereof, accept other categories of investments that comply with the principles of safety, profitability, liquidity, diversification and dispersal referred to above, and also grant derogations to the rules on the location of assets.

3. The regulations set maximum percentages for certain assets or groups of assets.

Moreover, no more than 5 per cent of the assets representing an insurer's technical provisions and liabilities may consist of investments in equities or other money market or capital instruments from a single issuer, or of loans to a single borrower, taken in the aggregate. A number of exceptions are provided for, however.

4. The regulations also set the rules for estimating the value of assets.

D. The profitability of products

Belgium believes that judicious rating is the best guarantee of the financial soundness of a company and consequently of its solvency. In the long term, a company cannot set aside sufficient assets nor increase its solvency margin unless it receives adequate premiums.

The regulations regarding the content and practical organisation of the supervision of profitability are explained in appendix.

E. Shareholders and the management of insurance companies

Recently, legislation has focused closely upon shareholders and the management of companies, and standards have been set for the professional ethics and qualifications of executives.

F. Reinsurance

At the time of licensing, companies must provide information concerning the method of reinsurance and the names of reinsurers. Any subsequent changes must be reported.

II. Practical organisation of supervision

The supervisory authority is the Office of Insurance Supervision.

Financial supervision is conducted on the basis of the following documents:

- the annual accounts, including the balance sheet, the profit and loss account, notes on the accounts and an itemised breakdown of the profit and loss account;
- the annual statement of the solvency margin constituted, together with an estimate of the margin to be constituted;
- statistics to be provided for each category of products, for purposes of supervising profitability and technical provisions (including the amount of annual benefits and provisions for claims);
- information on the technical basis for calculating premiums and technical provisions for life insurance;
- regarding asset valuation: companies must keep an ongoing record of the assets for each separate branch and file a statement of asset valuation for each type of investment with the Office of Insurance Supervision by 31 December of each

year. Furthermore, at the end of each quarter, the company must report any changes regarding the assets allotted to each separate branch, as well as an estimate of the amount of technical provisions.

In addition to examining data from companies, on-site inspections are conducted. The inspectors appointed by the Office must be provided with all information and documents enabling them to determine whether licensed companies are complying with the laws and regulations.

In addition to supervision by these inspectors, who are part of the regular staff of the Office, audits are conducted by auditors appointed by the supervisory authorities, under the supervision of the Office. These auditors report on the financial situation and management of companies at the request of the Office or at least once yearly.

Since 1991, the Insurance Supervision Act has required insurance companies to designate one or more actuaries who must be consulted with respect to rating, reinsurance and the amount of technical provisions or reserves. Their opinions may be of assistance to the supervisory authority.

In addition, life insurance regulations require that an actuary prepare an annual report to the supervisory authority, indicating theoretical surrender values, the present value of insured benefits, zillmerisation values, valuation reserves and technical provisions broken down into mathematical balance sheet provisions, dividend funds and provisions for benefits to be paid out, as well as the information needed to justify any difference between mathematical balance sheet provisions and valuation reserves.

III. Measures taken when difficulties arise (recovery measures)

If a company is not complying with the requirements for technical provisions and the corresponding assets, the Office of Supervision can restrict or prohibit the free disposal of assets. It can also require the company to increase its technical provisions and can take any additional steps required to protect the interests of insurance buyers, policyholders and beneficiaries.

In order to enable a company to recover when its solvency margin no longer meets the minimum limit, the Office requires that the company submit a recovery plan, and if it does not, the Office will impose its own plan. If the Office deems that the company's position is going to deteriorate further, it can restrict or prohibit the free disposal of assets.

If a solvency margin falls below the level of the guarantee fund (one-third of the margin, at the very least), the Office requires the company to submit a short-term financing plan. The Office can restrict or prohibit the company's free disposal of its assets and take any additional steps required to protect the interests of policyholders and beneficiaries.

When the Office of Insurance Supervision finds that a company is not operating in accordance with the law or regulations, that poor management or a weak financial situation is threatening its ability to meet its commitments or that its management or accounting system or its internal monitoring has serious defects, it sets time limits within which the situation must be corrected. If this is not done, the Office of Insurance Supervision may:

- appoint a special auditor;
- prohibit certain transactions or restrict business activities;
- transfer some or all of its policies to another company;
- require that managers, board members or general authorised agents be replaced within specified time limits, and if they are not, replace the entire management staff of the company by a provisional manager who will have complete authority to manage the company.

When the performance of a company is such that the interests of policyholders and beneficiaries are jeopardised, the Office of Supervision may make recommendations to the company regarding the advisability of a merger with or sale to a licensed company.

The Office of Supervision can also require that a company adjust a tariff appropriately if it observes that the tariff is causing the company to incur losses.

Lastly, its licence may be revoked by royal decree, on recommendation of the Office of Supervision, if a company:

- no longer meets the initial operating requirements;
- is seriously in breach of the regulations, especially with regard to the constitution of technical provisions or reserves and the corresponding assets;
- was unable to meet the time limit for compliance with the provisions of the recovery or financing plan.

The revocation can apply either to all branches of insurance written by the company or to one or several of them.

The licence is automatically revoked in the event of the bankruptcy or liquidation of a company. This revocation applies to all branches of insurance written.

Annex to the Note by the Belgian Delegation Concerning Insurance Supervision

I.   Introduction

Since 1975 the Office of Insurance Supervision (*Office de contrôle des assurances,* OCA) has overseen the solvency of insurance companies. In fact, supervises the overall solvency of companies even though solvency margins are calculated separately for life and non-life insurance.

However, the solvency margin does not provide an absolute guarantee of solvency. It is calculated on the basis of premiums, which means that when the volume of premiums is low, the margin will be small. Furthermore, it is not possible to determine the causes of an insurance company's difficulties or to evaluate its medium and long-term prospects on the basis of the solvency margin.

II.   Rates

Prior to July 1991, rates were not subject to prior approval. They were approved on a rule-of-thumb basis since the statistics needed to calculate the technically correct premium for each risk were not available.

Nevertheless, this procedure rarely gave rise to problems:

- there were almost no bankruptcies;
- there was an imposed rate for certain small risks (*i.e.,* auto insurance);
- there were market agreements;
- in branches where there was systematic under-pricing, losses were offset by the profits from other life or non-life branches.

This situation is likely to change fundamentally over the next few years because of increased competition. As insurance companies are forced to become more competitive, there will be pressure on them to pare rates to the minimum in a number of branches.

For this reason, there was a need to reinforce rate supervision; this could only be done retrospectively, by examining companies' results.

Consequently, the law on supervision was amended on 19 July 1991. The new legislation confirmed the principle of retrospective supervision. Moreover, Article 21a now makes it possible for the Office to require an insurance company to raise its rates if they are shown to be unprofitable.

III. General principles

It is a basic principle of business that a company cannot sell its products at a loss. Furthermore, each product should be profitable in its own right. Although a company will not necessarily fail because it is undercharging for a given product, it is unacceptable that policyholders in one branch should cover systematically the losses of another branch.

Property-priced products are the best guarantee of the financial soundness of a company and therefore of its solvency. In the long term, a company cannot build up substantial reserves nor maintain its solvency margin unless it charges adequate premiums.

If supervision is limited only to the company's overall financial situation, then, as in the past, problems will not detected until it is already too late or until they can only be solved by issuing new equity.

Supervision of the profitability of products is an extremely effective way of getting companies to do something about excessively low rates before their overall situation deteriorates. This does not necessarily mean that they have to raise rates. Other measures can be considered (*i.e.,* changes in the terms of insurance or their acceptance policies, tighter control of certain costs, etc.).

The profitability of products is generally calculated without taking into account income from free assets and deferred (unrealised) capital gains. However, elements such as capital gains realised on investments and depreciation or transfers of depreciation on investment property should be included.

The analysis should be as factual as possible. Profitability should be examined over a number of years, taking into account the specific characteristics of the company in question, the business climate, and the exceptional or recurrent nature of certain events. If necessary, the measures needed to redress the situation can be taken gradually so as not to create insurmountable difficulties in the short term.

IV. Implementing supervision of profitability

The tremendous diversity of insurance products makes it impossible to supervise the profitability of each individual product. Even if this were possible, the results would often have little significance because of the small number of contracts written for some risks.

Consequently, the Office decided to concentrate on the largest categories of contracts in each insurance class (*i.e.,* home fire insurance, personal life insurance Classes 21, 22 and 26, etc.).

Profitability is analysed using statistics for 33 categories of non-life products and 7 life products.

The attached table shows the different headings which make it possible to analyse the profitability of all the categories mentioned above.

The key item is the *gross technical-financial balance.* The gross reinsurance balance was selected because for many categories of products, reinsurance data are either non-existent or unreliable.

This emphasis on the gross balance does not mean that no interest is taken in the reinsurance ceded. Reinsurance should play its "normal" role (for example, it would be absurd to require a balanced gross technical-financial balance in a year in which a major catastrophe was totally covered in a reinsurance treaty; that said, it is absolutely necessary to re-establish profitability when a company resorts to reinsurance to offset a structural deficit on a category of products).

The following additional information is also relevant:

– *Operating costs*

Companies are required to break these costs down among the various categories of insurance products and to provide the Office with documentation supporting the breakdown. It proved impossible to provide the companies with clear-cut rules in this regard.

– *Technical reserves*

It is important to have an accurate idea of the "normal" amount of these reserves in order to calculate the profitability of categories of products with accuracy. In addition to carrying out on-site inspections, the Office requires companies to complete a detailed annual questionnaire regarding its methods of building up reserves. Furthermore, new statistical documents include more information on loss reserves (especially per underwriting year and, in general, per 10-year period).

– *Financial yields*

The Office has developed a standard method for calculating the financial yield on each category of insurance product. It is in fact an overall method. A rate of return is calculated by dividing all financial earnings by all of a company's assets (without distinguishing between representative assets and other assets, or between life and non-life business). The rate obtained is applied to the amount of technical reserves for each category of insurance product.

However, companies are free to choose another method as long as it complies with the principles explained above (see Section III). If necessary the Office will analyse any significant difference between the results obtained using the Office's method and that of the company.

– *The accounting year and the underwriting year*

During an initial phase, only the results of the accounting year will be examined. However, the ultimate goal is to refine the analysis so that conclusions can be reached and measures taken on the basis of the underwriting year.

– *Direct business in Belgium*

Current statistics only allow the supervisory authorities to analyse the profitability of categories of products for direct insurance operations in Belgium.

It is planned to expand the statistics so as to be able to carry out the same kind of study for accepted reinsurance and for insurance activities abroad (whether or not the company has an establishment abroad).

ITEMS STUDIED FOR THE CONTRIOL OF PROFITABILITY

			Code (Breakdown of Annual Accounts, Chapitre II, Section I)
	I.	**Premiums and charges**	
+	1.1.	Premiums written and remaining to be written	$002 + 004 - 0$
		a) Amount of premiums subject to contribution to the Belgian National Sickness and Invalidity Insurance Institute (I.N.A.M.I.)	
+	1.2.	Policy and endorsement costs	006
	II.	**Payments, refunds and handling of claims**	
	2.1.	Direct payments to beneficiaries	032
–	2.2.	External costs of settling claims	033
–	2.3.	Internal costs of settling claims	$(149) - (148)$
+	2.4.	Technical charges refunded	021
	III.	**Technical reserves and estimated refunds**	
+	3.1.	Reserves for unexpired risks, outstanding claims and probable losses, beginning of year	009
		a) Reserves for unexpired risks and outstanding claims	
		b) Reserve for probable losses	
–	3.2.	Reserves for unexpired risks, outstanding claims and probable losses, end of year	010
		a) Reserves for unexpired risks and outstanding claims	
		b) Reserve for probable losses	
	3.3.	Reserves for unexpired risks, outstanding claims and probable losses transferred	
+		*a)* Received	012
–		*b)* Ceded	013
+	3.4.	Reserve for claims admitted but not paid, beginning of year	041
		a) Reported claims reserve	
		b) IBNR claims reserve	
		c) Reserve for internal costs of settling claims	
–	3.5.	Reserve for claims admitted but not paid, end of business year	040
		a) Reported claims reserve	
		b) IBNR claims reserve	
		c) Reserve for internal costs of settling claims	
	3.6.	Reserve for claims admitted but not paid transferred	
+		*a)* Received	056
–		*b)* Ceded	055
	3.7.	Estimate of technical charges refunded	
–		*a)* Beginning of year	024
+		*b)* End of year	023
+	3.8.	Equalisation or balancing reserve, beginning of year	(053)
–	3.9.	Equalisation or balancing reserve, end of year	(052)

			Code (Breakdown of Annual Accounts, Chapitre II, Section I)
	3.10.	Equalisation reserve transferred	( )
+		a) Received	
−		b) Ceded	
+	3.11.	Other technical reserves, beginning of year	(053)
		a) Reserve for increasing age	
		b) Other reserves	
−	3.12.	Other technical reserves, end of year	(052)
		a) Reserve for increasing age	
		b) Other reserves	
	3.13.	Other technical reserves transferred	( )
+		a) Received	
−		b) Ceded	

IV. Other technical charges and earnings

−	4.1.	Other technical charges	065
+	4.2.	Other technical income	( )

V. Dividends and refunds

−	5.1.	Amount allotted for the year to the dividend reserve	058
−	5.2.	Dividends paid	
		a) From the previous year's reserve	062
		b) From the current year's reserve	063
	5.3.	Dividend reserve	
+		a) Beginning of year	(053)
−		b) End of year	(052)
	5.4.	Dividend reserve transferred	( )
+		a) Received	
−		b) Ceded	

VI. Acquisition costs and commissions

−	6.1.	Commissions	068 + 069 − 070 + 071
−	6.2.	Acquisition costs	(149) − (148)

GROSS BALANCE OF INSURANCE ACTIVITY

VII. Administrative costs

−	7.	Administrative costs	(149) − (148)

GROSS BALANCE BEFORE INVESTMENT EARNINGS

VIII. Investment earnings

	8.1.	Earnings from dividends and other investments	(144)
+	8.2.	Transfers of adjustments of value of investments	(154)
+	8.3.	Realised capital gains	(162)

IX. Investment costs

	9.1.	Interest charges	(145)
−	9.2.	Investment management charges	( )
−	9.3.	Adjustments of value of investments	(157)
−	9.4.	Realised capital losses	(165)

GROSS TECHNICAL-FINANCIAL BALANCE

X. Reinsurance ceded

	10.	Balance of reinsurance ceded	115 – 130
+			

NET TECHNICAL-FINANCIAL BALANCE

XI. Allocation of non-technical income (net of charges) to categories of insurance products

XII. Allocation of deferred capital gains on investments to categories of insurance products

XIII. Allocation of deferred capital losses on investments to categories of insurance products

CANADA

The following provides a general overview of the regulatory regime in Canada. A more detailed discussion of the subject as respects life insurance companies was presented to members of the OECD Insurance Solvency Committee at their inaugural meeting on 22 April 1993.

I. Regulatory framework and supervisory approach

A. *Canadian insurance industry*

The Canadian insurance industry consists of both Canadian incorporated insurers (either federally or provincially) and insurers incorporated outside Canada. The Canadian market is dominated by deferally incorporated insurers (''Canadian companies'') and by foreign insurers operating a branch in Canada (''foreign companies''). Provincially incorporated insurers represent only 5 per cent of the market.

The federal and provincial governments share responsibility for insurance regulation in Canada. Federal authorities are responsible for ensuring the solvency of Canadian companies and the Canadian branch operations of foreign companies. Provincial authorities are responsible for reviewing and interpreting insurance contracts, licensing and supervising agents and ensuring the solvency of provincially incorporated insurers. In addition to becoming federally registered, a Canadian company or foreign company must also be licensed in every province and territory where it proposes to carry on business (there are 10 provinces and 2 territories, each with their own governing statute).

B. *Regulatory authority*

The office of the Superintendent of Financial Institutions (''OSFI''), a federal department, is the primary regulator of insurance companies in Canada. OSFI also regulates banks, federally incorporated trust and loan companies, investment companies and pension plans of federally regulated industries. The Superintendent of Financial Institutions reports to the Minister of Finance.

OSFI is charged with the administration of the Insurance Companies Act (''ICA''), a federal statute applicable to life and non-life Canadian and foreign insurance companies. The rules are basically the same for all companies; the main difference is that foreign companies are required to vest in trust in Canada Assets to cover their Canadian liabilities plus a margin. There are no significant differences in the rules applicable to direct writers and professional reinsurers.

The ICA contains provisions governing the incorporation and registration of Canadian and foreign companies, the capital structure and corporate governance of Canadian companies, the business and powers of Canadian Companies, the investment rules, capital adequacy rules and self-dealing rules applicable to Canadian and foreign companies, and the filing requirements applicable to Canadian and foreign companies. The ICA also gives the Superintendent broad discretion to issue directions of compliance, to impose restrictions on a company's authority to insure risks, and to take control of a company or its assets where circumstances warrant.

C. Control of entry

The ability to maintain regulatory control over new entrants is a key element in ensuring the health of the Canadian insurance industry. The ICA sets out certain factors that the Minister must take into account before issuing letters patent incorporating a Canadian insurance company. These factors include the nature and sufficiency of the financial resources of the applicant as a source of continuing financial support for the new company, the soundness and feasibility of the company's business plans, the business record and experience of the applicants, the competence and experience of company management, and the best interests of the financial system in Canada. The ICA stipulates that a new Canadian company must have at least C$10 million of capital or such higher amount as the Minister may require before commencing business.

In practice, the Office requires that the amount of initial capital be adequate to meet the new company's needs for the first three to five years. In addition, a company specialising in reinsurance or some other specialty class like title insurance or mortgage insurance must have more capital than the statutory minimum. The Office routinely obtains police reports on directors and senior officials of a proposed new company.

A foreign company wishing to carry on insurance in Canada on a branch basis must first obtain the approval of the Minister. Before granting approval, the Minister must be satisfied that the foreign company is capable of making a contribution to the financial system in Canada.

There are several criteria that must be met before the Office would be prepared to consider an application by a foreign insurer for registration in Canada. The applicant must have assets of at least C$200 million, capital of between 5 per cent and 10 per cent of liabilities, and a successful record of operations in its home jurisdiction. In addition, the Office must be satisfied that the company's business plans for Canada are acceptable and that the company will maintain adequate records in Canada.

D. Changes in ownership

Control on entry to the Canadian financial system is meaningless without similar controls on changes in ownership. The ICA stipulates that where more than 10 per cent of any class of shares of a company is purchased or otherwise acquired, the prior approval of the Minister is required. Any change in the control of a company is very significant to the regulator. Such situations are reviewed in much the same way as a new incorporation.

E. Fundamental changes

Demutualization, amalgamation, and business transfers are all fundamental changes which can impact on the financial health of a company and consequently require the prior approval of the Minister. In most situations, the ICA requires that an independent actuary report on the transaction and that the policyholders be informed.

It is standard practice for the Office to request detailed proforma statements showing the effect of the proposed transaction on the parties involved. Considerable reliance is placed on the opinion of the independent actuary. The Office would not likely support any transaction that would adversely affect policyholders of either company.

F. Capital adequacy – Life companies

The ICA requires Canadian life companies to maintain adequate capital, and adequate and appropriate forms of liquidity, and to comply with any regulations made in this regard. No regulations have been proclaimed to date, however, companies are expected to follow the Minimum Continuing Capital and Surplus Requirements (''MCCSR'') first issued by OSFI in October 1992 in the form of a draft guideline. The capital adequacy rules for life companies will remain in the form of a guideline for the foreseeable future for greater flexibility.

MCCSR measures the capital required by a company against the capital it has available as at a certain date. The amount of capital required is based on a risk weight system similar to that in place for banks. The main difference is that, in the case of life companies, factors are applied to both assets and liabilities. The elements of capital acceptable to meet requirements are similar to those applicable to banks; two tiers of capital are acceptable, tier 1 consisting of capital with the most permanence and having no fixed interest or dividend charges. All capital must be subordinate to policyholder obligations.

The Superintendent may, by order, direct a company to maintain more capital than required under the MCCSR guideline. If a company's capital falls below 100 per cent of its capital requirements, the Superintendent must report the situation to the Minister.

Similar rules apply to foreign life companies in respect of their Canadian business. They are required to maintain an adequate margin of assets in Canada over liabilities in Canada, and adequate and appropriate forms of liquidity, and to comply with any regulations made in this regard. For foreign companies, MCCSR measures the assets required to be maintained in Canada against the assets available in Canada.

In practice, the Office requires life companies to maintain capital at 120 per cent MCCSR. Companies falling below this level will be asked to submit business plans showing the measures to be taken to restore capital to acceptable levels, will be subject to more frequent reporting, more frequent examinations, and in general, stricter monitoring.

G. Capital adequacy – Non-life companies

The ICA requires non-life companies to maintain assets equal to their policy and other liabilities plus a margin equal to the greatest of the results of three calculations using: 1) unearned premiums and unpaid claims, 2) premiums written, 3) claims incurred over three years. These rules, which have been in place for several years, are spelled out in regulations. As in the case of life companies, the Superintendent may, by order, direct a company to increase its assets above the level required by the regulations. The sanctions against a company that fails to comply with the capital adequacy rules are the same as for a life company. The same rules apply to foreign non-life companies in respect of the assets they maintain in Canada to cover their Canadian liabilities.

H. Financial reporting

The ICA stipulates that company shall provide the Superintendent with such information, at such times and in such form as the Superintendent may require. This gives the Superintendent maximum flexibility. The ICA also sets out the type of information required as part of an annual return and the deadline for filing such return. Canadian companies and foreign companies alike must file audited returns. In addition, the return is not complete unless accompanies by the report of the appointed actuary.

In practice, all non-life companies are required to submit quarterly financial statements. Newly incorporated life companies and problem companies are required to file quarterly statements. Special filings are required on an *ad hoc* basis; for example, during the Olympia and York crisis, companies were asked to list all their holdings in corporations affiliated with O & Y. Presently, all non-life companies file their annual and interim return data on diskette in addition to hard copy.

I. On-site examinations

The ICA requires the Superintendent to cause an examination or enquiry to be made into the business and affairs of each company at least once a year or, if circumstances warrant, less frequently, but not less frequently than once every two years. The stated purpose of the examination is to satisfy the Superintendent that the company is complying with the Act and is in a sound financial condition.

The Office has four regional examination offices across Canada. For the most part, companies are examined every two years by a team of OSFI examiners assisted by actuarial staff and on occasion, by outside credit consultants. The examination concentrates on those risk areas identified by Office staff in a pre-examination analysis of the company. The examiners also rely on the work of the external auditor. Where an insurance company is part of a conglomerate involving other federally regulated financial institutions, for example, banks or trust or loan companies, every effort is made to co-ordinate an examination of all federally regulated institutions at the same time. In addition, the Office tries to ensure the sharing of pertinent information among staff responsible for supervision companies in a conglomerate. Examination results are incorporated in a monthly report to the Minister on problem companies.

J. Remedial powers

One of the remedial powers available to the Superintendent is the issuance of a direction of compliance where a company or a person connected to a particular company, such as an officer or director, is committing or is about to commit an act that is unsafe or unsound or is pursuing or is about to pursue a course of conduct that is unsafe or unsound. The company or person to whom the direction of compliance is directed is normally given an opportunity to make representations before the direction is issued. However, the Superintendent may issue a temporary direction which has immediate effect if the Superintendent believes that the circumstances warrant. This power has seldom been used. The threat of issuing such an order is often sufficient to correct the unsafe or unsound practice.

II. Supervising problem companies

A. Early warning systems

Over the years OSFI has developed a comprehensive procedure for identifying potential problem companies and action plans for dealing with such companies. OSFI reports to the Minister every month on problem companies outlining the problems and the proposed action. Some of the factors used in identifying problem companies are:

- incomplete filings;
- MCCSR less than 120 per cent;(life companies);
- asset margin 10 per cent (non-life companies);
- owners unable or unwilling to inject capital;
- weak management/inadequate internal controls;
- parent or affiliate in difficulty;
- inadequate or aggressive premium rates;
- succession of operating losses;
- lack of experience in new lines of business;
- material change in senior management;
- inadequate claims or policy reserves;
- high overhead expenses;
- questionable reinsurance arrangements;
- inadequate records;
- regulatory action taken in home jurisdiction.

B. Remedial actions

Once a company is identified as a problem company OSFI may take action as follows depending on the nature and severity of the problem:

- monitor company more closely;
- require company to tile business plans and interim statements;
- conduct a special on-site examination;
- hire credit consultants to apprise asset portfolio;

- request additional capital or assets in Canada;
- issue a direction of compliance for unsafe or unsound business practice;
- restrict company's premium volume, investment activity or investing or lending operations.

The ICA provides that where the Superintendent is of the opinion that the assets of the company are not satisfactorily accounted or are not sufficient to give adequate protection to all the policyholders and creditors of the company, or that there exists any practice or state of affairs that is materially prejudicial to the interests of policyholders or creditors, or where the company has failed to pay any liability that has become due, the Superintendent may immediately take control of the assets of the company and maintain control for seven days or such longer periods as the Minister considers necessary to enable the company to make representations. In practice, the company is given ample opportunity to make representations before the Superintendent intervenes.

The ICA requires the Superintendent to report to the Minister where the Superintendent has taken control of a company's assets, where the company's capital or assets fall below the level required by the ICA or where the Superintendent is of the opinion that the company's assets are not sufficient to provide adequate protection to policyholders and creditors. After giving the company an opportunity to make representations, the Minister may:

- place terms and conditions on the company's operations;
- set a time period for correcting the problems;
- direct the Superintendent to take control of the company (control of the assets of a foreign company);
- while the Superintendent has control, request the Attorney General to apply for a winding-up order against the company.

The winding-up of a company is a last resort. OSFI will make every effort to assist the company in a reorganisation or restructuring to correct the problems. However, if it becomes obvious that the company cannot be saved then immediate action will be taken to prevent further loss to policyholders and creditors.

DENMARK

I. Supervisory rules – the Danish act on insurance business

The Act, which applies to all insurance business (both direct insurance and reinsurance), has been adapted to existing EU Directives and incorporates rules which to a great extent are common to non-life insurance business and life insurance business. The two forms of business cannot be carried on by the same company. It should be noted, however, that at the time of writing (February 1995) work is in progress on a proposal permitting life insurance companies to carry on non-life insurance business within classes 1 and 2 (Accident and Sickness) in accordance with Article 13(2) of the First Life Insurance Coordination Directive as amended by Article 16 of the Third Life Insurance Coordination Directive.

The insurance business may be carried on by public limited companies, by mutual companies where the policyholders are the owners and only members of the company, and by certain pension funds (''tværgånde pensionskasser'') comprised by the Act.

The right of foreign insurance companies to carry on business in Denmark is described below in Section II.A.1*b)* and *c)*.

A large number of administrative rules have been laid down in relation to the Act.

II. Supervision

The Danish Financial Supervisory Authority is responsible for the public supervision of insurance activities in Denmark.

A. *Authorization and solvency control*

1. *Authorization*

a) Insurance companies with head office in Denmark

The company must have permission authorization – from the Danish Financial Supervisory Authority to carry on insurance business. A company is entitled to receive the authorization without any limitation in time if it satisfies the conditions of the Danish Act on Insurance Business and an application for registration has been filed with the

Danish Commerce and Companies Agency. The authorization will be valid for – at least – the entire EEA and it will permit the company to carry on business there under either the right of establishment or the freedom to provide services.

Any application for authorization must be accompanied by, among other things, a memorandum of association, a scheme of operations and information about anyone holding directly or indirectly at least 10 per cent of the capital or the voting rights or having a holding which makes it possible to exercise a significant influence over the operations of the insurance company as well as information about the size of the holding of these capital owners.

If an application is filed for authorization to effect life and pension assurance, the general technical basis, etc., is to be notified to the Danish Financial Supervisory Authority on or before the day on which the technical basis etc. begins to be used. The same applies to any subsequent change in the mentioned circumstances.

Special rules apply to compulsory workmen's compensation insurance as no authorization may be issued until the Danish Financial Supervisory Authority has approved the general insuranceconditions and technical basis of the insurance company (*cf.* also below).

b) Foreign insurance companies with head office in another country within the EU or in another country within the EEA

A foreign insurance company having been granted authorization in another country within the European Union or in another country within the EEA, may carry on business in Denmark through a branch and/or through the provision of cross-frontier services when the Danish Financial Supervisory Authority has received the documentation, including a solvency certificate, prescribed by the Third Non-life Insurance Coordination Directive and the Third Life Insurance Coordination Directive from the supervisory authorities of the home country.

As regards workmen's compensation insurance, the rules laid down in the not Third Non-life Insurance Business do apply to such business carried on in exclusion provision (Article 49) in the Directive concerned: ''The Kingdom of Denmark may postpone until 1 January 1999 the application of this Directive to compulsory insurance against accidents at work. During that period the exclusion provided for in Article 12(2) of Directive 88/357/EEC for accidents at work shall continue to apply in the Kingdom of Denmark.''

c) Foreign insurance companies with head office in a country outside the EU or in a country outside the EEA

Such a foreign insurance company which lawfully carries on insurance business in its home country may be granted permission – authorization – by the Danish Financial Supervisory Authority to carry on similar business in Denmark through a local branch subject to certain specified conditions. One is that Danish companies shall be granted a similar right in the country concerned.

2.   Solvency control

According to the Insurance Business Act an insurance company must have a certain basic capital in order to carry on insurance business. The basic capital required is determined by calculating the company's solvency margin. The basic capital must constitute at least the same amount as the solvency margin.

The Danish rules concerning calculation of the solvency margin comply strictly with the rules of the EU Directives on Non-life Insurance and the Directives on Life Insurance.

The basic capital is calculated on the basis of the company's capital and reserves with various additions and deductions.

The rules concerning the elements of the basic capital have been changed in various respects in connection with the implementation of the Third Non-life Insurance Coordination Directive and the Third Life Insurance Coordination Directive.

Of elements that can be added now can be mentioned:

Subordinated capital contributions (subordinated loan capital) which meet certain specified conditions. The addition must not exceed an amount equal to 50 per cent of the solvency margin.

Members' accounts in mutual companies and in certain pension funds ("tværgånde pensionskasser") covered by the Insurance Business Act if the mentioned accounts satisfy certain specified conditions.

According to the Insurance Business Act, the companies must submit their annual accounts to the Danish Financial Supervisory Authority. In this connection, the companies must fill in a special form which shows how the solvency margin has been calculated, as well as submit a statement showing the amount and composition of the basic capital. This enables the Danish Financial Supervisory Authority to check the existence and adequacy of the basic capital.

If the basic capital is not sufficient, a number of measures are available to the Danish Financial Supervisory Authority.

Foreign insurance companies having their head office in another country within the EU or the EEA, (cf. II.A.1b) above), are not required to possess in Denmark any basic capital to cover the solvency margin. Instead, a solvency certificate issued by the supervisory authority in the country in which the company has its head office is required.

Neither is the company required in Denmark to be in possession of funds to cover its commitments under insurance contracts effected in Denmark.

Foreign insurance companies having their head office in a country outside the EU or the EEA, (cf. II.A.1c) above), must possess assets in Denmark for the coverage of the solvency margin required (not less than one half of the minimum amount fixed for domestic companies). Deposits are required and the deposits are normally amounting to $1/4$ of the minimum amount of the solvency margin calculated as for domestic companies.

In addition, the company must possess sufficient funds in Denmark to meet its commitments under direct insurance contracts effected in Denmark.

However, it should be noted that non-life insurance companies having their head office in Switzerland are subject to the rules laid down in the "Swiss Agreement" if such a company wants to carry on business in Denmark through a branch. This means that a solvency certificate from the Swiss supervisory authorities replaces the demand for funds in Denmark to cover the solvency margin.

3. Investment rules

In connection with the implementation of the Third Non-life Insurance Coordination Directive and the Third Life Insurance Coordination Directive, new investment rules have been laid down for insurance companies and certain pension funds ("tværgånde pensionskasser") covered by the Insurance Business Act. The rules came into operation on 1 July 1994.

The rules in force until 1 July 1994 were characterised by two main principles:

– At least 60 per cent of the life insurance provisions/provisions for unearned premiums and outstanding claims were to be placed in the socalled "gilt-edged" assets (*e.g.* government bonds (Danish or foreign), certain other high security bonds, deposits in credit institutions and real property). The remaining 40 per cent was not subject to any investment requirements.
– The rule concerning restrictions on the size of any one investment. In the field of life insurance the limit was fixed at 2 per cent of the balance sheet total and applied to the investments of all companies. In the field of non-life insurance the limit was 4 per cent of the insurance provisions and applied only to the assets that corresponded to the insurance provisions.

These two main principles have in all essentials been preserved, (*cf.,* however, the changes mentioned below).

In accordance with the Directives the Danish investment rules lay down:

– Investment principles to be incorporated by the companies into their investment policy within the applicable investment rules.
– An exhaustive list of admissible types of assets.
– Limits to the extent of investments in certain types of assets.
– Limits to the amount of any one investment.

a) Investment principles

The general investment principles stipulate that the type and composition of the assets applied in covering insurance provisions must be such that they can satisfy the insured in terms of **security, return** and **liquidity**. There must be no disproportionate dependence on a certain category of assets, a certain investment market or a certain investment.

b) List of assets

The list of admissible types of assets contains a more detailed description of categories of assets than the list of assets in the Directives. The reason for this is a desire to make the list suitable as a frame of reference for the fixing of investment limits.

c) Limits for types of assets

The rules lay down the following limits for investments in certain types of assets:

– Non-"gilt-edged" assets   max. 40 per cent;
– Unlisted securities   max. 10 per cent;
– Listed securities from countries outside Zone A   max. 10 per cent;
– Unsecured unlisted loans (not more than 1 per cent
  per debtor)   max. 2 per cent.

(Zone A is a category of countries laid down by a Directive, comprising the OECD countries and Saudi Arabia.)

"Gilt-edged" assets are government and mortgage credit bonds, properties, bank deposits, secured mortgages, etc. The most important asset of the non-"gilt-edged" assets is shares.

The mentioned limit of 40 per cent for non-"gilt-edged" assets corresponds to the previous 60 per cent rule, according to which at least 60 per cent of the funds were to be invested in "gilt-edged" assets.

All the limits are applied in relation to the size of the insurance provisions for own account.

d) Limits for any one investment

The current limit within non-life insurance according to which not more than 4 per cent of the insurance provisions may be placed in any one enterprise has been maintained.

Within life insurance there is a limit of 3 per cent of the insurance provisions for investments in any one enterprise. However, this limit is only applicable if the enterprise in which the investment is to be made has its head office and is quoted on the stock exchange in a country inside Zone A and has capital and reserves of not less than DKr 250 million. Otherwise the limit is 2 per cent.

In addition to the generally applicable limits for any one investment, a number of other limits have been fixed for special investments, namely:

– Any one property   max. 5 per cent;
– Minority holding in a property company   max. 5 per cent;
– A subsidiary under supervision (bank-insurance mortgage
  credit)   max. 5 per cent;
– Mortgage credit bonds per issuer   max. 40 per cent;
– Deposits with banks and bank or insurance guaranteed
  claims per institute or insurance company   max. 10 per cent;

– Investment association units per association or division
thereof   max. 10 per cent.

e) Consolidated approach (look – through principle) for certain subsidiaries

Certain subsidiaries are subject to special rules, according to which the underlying assets of the subsidiary may be treated directly as part of the assets covering the parent company's provisions. By way of example, the ownership of a property subsidiary is not treated as a share investment but as a property investment.

Such a consolidated approach can be applied in relation to the following types of subsidiaries:
– Investment subsidiaries, *i.e.* subsidiaries whose only activity is to invest in and manage such assets as are covered by the list of assets.
– Insurance subsidiaries. The assets of the subsidiary to which the rule can be applied are limited to assets which are not applied in covering the subsidiary's own insurance provisions. Moreover, the subsidiary's solvency margin must be deducted. If the subsidiary is a non-life insurance company, however, its assets can only be applied in this way within a limit of 5 per cent of the parent company's provisions.

III. Circumstances, forms and consequences of suspension and cessation of business

Suspension and cessation of the business of a company imply, in that order, suspension or cessation of the issue of new policies. Suspension and cessation may be voluntary or compulsory, partial or total.

A.   *Voluntary suspension – total or partial*

The Insurance Business Act makes no direct provision for the situation in which a company wishes voluntary to suspend issue of contracts in some or all of the classes in which it carries on business. There is nothing to prevent it from doing this. It is nevertheless a condition of suspension that the company inform the supervisory authority.

Such notice does not entail withdrawal of the company's authorization, but the supervisory authority has the access to withdraw an authorization if the company has not used it for 2 years or more.

Voluntary suspension of the issue of contracts has no effect on contracts in force.

B.   *Voluntary cessation – total or partial*

If a company finally ceases issue of contracts in some or all of the classes in which it carries on business, the supervisory authority must be informed.

If the company ceases all issue of contracts and does not voluntarily transfer its portfolio within a reasonably short time, the supervisory authority normally asks that such a transfer be made or that the company go into liquidation. In the case of a life insurance company it may be that the company's life insurance portfolio will be placed under the administration of the supervisory authority.

Such cessation has no immediate effect on policies already issued.

C. Compulsory suspension – total or partial

If the financial circumstances and situation of a company are such that the interests of the insured are in danger, the supervisory authority may require as a provisional measure that the company suspends issue of policies in some or all the classes in which it is doing business (see *F.1.* below).

It is not necessary that such a requirement be published.

Suspension does not entail immediate withdrawal of the company's authorization.

If the situation of the company has changed so that the suspension is no longer necessary, the supervisory authority makes a statement to this effect.

If the opposite is the case, the suspension will short delay by the authorization and at from the supervisory authority that the company be wound up or, if it is a life insurance company, that its portfolio be placed under the administration of the supervisory authority. Compulsory suspension has no effect on insurance contracts in force.

D. Compulsory cessation – total or partial

If the financial situation and state of business of a company are such that the interests of the insured are endangered and the company does not take the measures which the supervisory authority has prescribed within the time that the supervisory authority allows for this, the latter may withdraw the company's authorization and at the same time may require that the company goes into liquidation and, if it is a life insurance company, it may take its portfolio under its administration.

In connection with any withdrawal of a company's authorization the supervisory authority may prohibit the free disposal of the assets of the company or may restrict – its free disposal of such assets.

As will be explained below in connection with administration of the portfolio of a life insurance company, Danish law endeavours to ensure that the life insurance contracts in question will be kept in force, if they have to be administered, as far as possible.

E. Company's right of appeal

A decision by the supervisory authority that a company must suspend business, go into liquidation (apart from bankruptcy), or be placed under administration may be submitted to the Danish Commerce and Companies Appeal Board at the latest 4 weeks after notice has been received of such decision. The decision of the supervisory authority and that of the appeal board may be taken before the courts. In the latter case, the time limit is 6 months.

F. Transfer of contracts and transfer of the company

1. Transfer of portfolio

- without corresponding assets and liabilities;
- with corresponding assets and liabilities.

If a company wishes voluntarily to transfer its whole portfolio or a specified part of it to another company it must make a request to this effect to the supervisory authority, attaching the proposed agreement between the two companies, and subsequently forwarding information about the companies enabling the supervisory authority to judge whether the transfer is without risk for the policyholders. If the supervisory authority is of the opinion that the transfer should be authorised, it must publish a report relating to the transfer and an invitation to the policyholders to inform it in writing within three months if they do not wish the transfer to be made. At the same time, the company must inform the policyholders directly. After the expiration of the time limit mentioned above, the supervisory authority, taking due account of any objections advanced, shall decide whether the insurance portfolio may be transferred in accordance with the proposal submitted. The transfer may not be pleaded as grounds for cancelling an insurance policy.

By virtue of rules similar to those mentioned above, two or more life insurance companies (or general insurance companies) may, for example, merge and form a new company.

It is not necessary to get the permission of the supervisory authority for the transfer if the insurance company in connection with the transfer obtains the consent of every single policyholder.

The compulsory transfer of the portfolio of one insurance company to another will be dealt with in more detail below in the chapter on winding-up. The portfolio may be transferred to another insurance company.

As mentioned earlier the Danish legislation requires specialisation between life insurance and non-life insurance (*cf.* yet Section I). This implies that a life insurance portfolio can only be transferred to another life insurance company and a non-life insurance portfolio to another nonlife insurance company.

A possibility is given to an insurance company to transform itself to a non-insurance company after having transferred all its insurance activity to another insurance company.

It has been a normal rule that an insurance company, which no longer carries on insurance activity, should be dissolved either by amalgamation or by voluntary or compulsory winding-up.

According to a special provision an insurance company, which has transferred its entire insurance portfolio to another insurance company according to the legal procedure, can no longer exist as an insurance company. If it is not dissolved by winding-up or special cases of amalgamation, the Danish Supervisory Authority of Financial Affairs shall approve the form and the content and the accomplishment of the liquidation as insurance company.

It means, for instance, that a limited insurance company having transferred its insurance activity can – if approved by the supervisory authority – remain as an ordinary limited company doing other business than insurance.

In so far the transfer has taken place to an insurance company being a subsidiary of the transferring company, the latter will then be a holding company for its insurance subsidiary.

2. Transfer of the company

Special rules are laid down in the case of amalgamation. These rules apply in the event of an insurance company wishing to transfer the whole of its assets and liabilities to another insurance company and if a decision is taken to amalgamate two or more insurance companies into a new insurance company. Such transfers are only valid with the permission of the supervisory authority.

The same proceedings concerning publication of the proposed agreement and the time limit given the policyholders as mentioned above shall apply. Furthermore, the supervisory authority shall be ascertained that the continuing company still has sufficient assets to cover the solvency margin and the technical reserves, taking account of the portfolio transferred to it.

G. Winding-up

If an insurance company is doing business in several classes of insurance, the fact that it ceases to issue contracts in some of these classes does not normally result in its winding-up.

If, on the other hand, the company completely ceases to issue new contracts, the consequence may be as was stated above, that its portfolio has to be transferred to another company (or, if it is a life insurance company, that its portfolio is placed under administration), and at the same time, that the company is required to go into liquidation.

1. The following rules apply to voluntary liquidation

The general meeting of an insurance company may, according to what its Articles of Association lay down in the matter, decide that the company should go into liquidation. If it is a life insurance company, it may not do so without the consent of all the individual policyholders unless it has first transferred its entire life insurance portfolio to another life insurance company in accordance with the relevant rules laid down by law, or unless at least its life insurance portfolio has been placed under administration.

In case of liquidation, the general meeting elects one or more liquidators for this purpose. It may also request the Probate Court to nominate liquidators, and the Minister of Business and Industry may also, if this seems justified to safeguard the interests of the insured, of shareholders, of guarantors or of creditors, nominate a liquidator to take charge of liquidation jointly with the liquidators elected by the general meeting.

The liquidators ensure that accounts closed at the time of liquidation are drawn up and made available to the insured, to shareholders, to guarantors and to creditors at the offices of the company as quickly as possible, and that a copy is also sent to the supervisory authority.

The liquidators must also, by means of a published notice, invite the creditors of the company to present their claims. After the assets have been distributed, the liquidators submit their final liquidation accounts to a general meeting and also forward them to the supervisory authority.

If it becomes clear during the winding-up that the circumstances which led to it have changed, it may be terminated and the company may begin business again when its balance sheet shows, in the opinion of the supervisory authority, that its liabilities are entirely covered and that the capital is sufficiently intact.

If the company's licence has been withdrawn, it cannot continue its activity, until a new licence has been granted.

2. *The following rules apply to compulsory winding-up*

   a) *Domestic general insurance companies*

Under more detailed provisions set out in the legislation, the supervisory authority has the power to decide that an insurance company shall go into liquidation. This is to be done in particular if the financial interests of the insured are in danger and if this danger has not been removed by other measures. If the supervisory authority has decided that a company is to be liquidated, the Probate Court, after consultation with the supervisory authority, nominates one or more liquidators. The Act lays down more detailed rules for the liquidation procedure. The supervisory authority, in consultation with the liquidators, examines whether it is expedient to transfer the whole or part of the portfolio to one or more insurance companies carrying on business in Denmark. If transfer takes place in accordance with the decision of the supervisory authority, the winding-up and the transfer cannot be pleaded as grounds for terminating an insurance contract.

   b) *Domestic life insurance companies*

In circumstances such as have been described above for general insurance companies the supervisory authority may decide to place the portfolio of a life insurance company under administration. In such cases, the right of the company to carry on life insurance business ceases, and the supervisory authority takes possession of all the company's assets registered to cover the life insurance provisions. These assets will thus be used exclusively to meet the claims of the insured.

Individual policyholders may not bring claims against the company. On the other hand, the supervisory authority acting on behalf of the estate under administration, may claim from the company any amount that may be shown by the valuation of the assets taken over to be needed to cover the life insurance provisions and insurance claims notified and due. Furthermore, the supervisory authority, acting on behalf of the estate under administration, may claim any amount corresponding to the basic capital that is equivalent to the solvency margin calculated for the company out of any moneys that may be in hand according to a balance sheet drawn up at the commencement of the administration procedure.

The supervisory authority shall as soon as possible seek to have the whole of the assurance portfolio taken over by one or more life insurance companies carrying on business in Denmark. If a take-over offer is received, the supervisory authority shall, if it finds the offer acceptable, prepare a report on the situation and a proposal for an agreement with the company in question.

The report and the proposal shall be published in the Danish Official Gazette and in daily newspapers, and in other appropriate manner, and shall contain an invitation to policyholders to inform the supervisory authority in writing within a time limit of at least one month if they have any objections to the transfer. At the same time, the company shall send a copy of the report and the proposal to policyholders whose addresses are known to it, making reference to the publication which has taken place and stating the date on which it took place.

When the time limit has expired, the supervisory authority, having due regard to any objections advanced, shall decide whether the assurance portfolio may be transferred as proposed. The transfer may not be pleaded as grounds for cancelling an assurance contract.

If the assurance portfolio cannot be transferred the supervisory authority shall convene a general meeting of the policyholders to form a mutual company. If a new company cannot be formed, the administration shall continue. As a general rule, the supervisory authority decides at the same time that the company shall go into liquidation.

An insurance company may be declared bankrupt. A petition in bankruptcy can be filed with the Probate Court either by the company itself or by creditors. If an insurance company becomes insolvent, the supervisory authority shall file a petition in bankruptcy with the Probate Court.

FINLAND

I. General

The insurance supervision is organised on the ministerial level as the Insurance Department in the Ministry of Social Affairs and Health, and the Insurance Department is also responsible for drafting the legislation on both private and social insurance. This has led to a collaboration between private and social insurance. As a consequence, a major part of social insurance is run by private insurers. This has also made possible that the benefits provided by certain private insurance (*e.g.* motor third party liability insurance, voluntary occupational pensions) have been adequately integrated with the corresponding benefits in the social insurance.

The supervision of the solvency of the insurers is based on the risk theory, which takes into account the stochastic nature of the insurance business. Thus the specific features such as the level of net retentions, the composition and the volume of the business and the risk of major nature catastrophes of each insurer have a central role in testing the solvency. The equalisation reserves are also based on the risk theory. Moreover, the calculation bases of the technical reserves are on a solid basis.

The role of the Ministry has been active in developing the insurance and has not been limited only to pure supervisory purposes. This applies especially to the compulsory insurance classes and the technical bases of insurance.

One form of the Finnish insurance inspection is to examine the information that the insurance concerns without request are obliged to submit to the supervisory authority. The Ministry can nevertheless require other information necessary for the supervision from the insurance concern. The other form of supervision is to carry out inspections in the insurance concerns and to be present at the meetings of a domestic company.

The manner in which to exercise the supervision is not regulated in detail. The limits of the contents of insurance inspection are stipulated by law, as well as the manners of supervision to be used. Within these limits and partly some more detailed rules the supervisory authority can choose the line of action which at the given time seems most appropriate.

The decentralised supervision of financial groups in accordance with the present legislation between the Bank of Finland, the Bank Inspectorate and the Ministry of Social Affairs and Health has not been seen as effective enough in supervision of financial groups and concentrations and a completely new supervisory body, a finance inspection, has been established. The finance inspection will have the main responsibility for supervision of financial groups in general. The tasks of the Bank Inspectorate will be transferred to that body, as well as certain supervisory tasks from the Bank of Finland. The finance inspection will follow, alongside with the Insurance Department of the Ministry of Social Affairs and Health, also investments of insurance institutions, where necessary, with a view to the supervision of risk concentrations in the financial markets. Enforceable decisions concerning investments of insurance companies will be taken by the Ministry of Social Affairs and Health also in the future, however.

The current Finnish rules on insurance supervision are mainly contained in the Insurance Companies Act and in the Decree concerning the Ministry of Social Affairs and Health. A foreign insurance company has the right to transact insurance business in Finland by establishing an agency as provided in the Act on Operations of Foreign Insurance Companies in Finland. If a foreign insurance company wishes to establish a subordinated company in Finland, the Insurance Companies Act shall apply (current changes due to the EEA Agreement).

Today the Finnish insurance supervision covers all classes of insurance and, as far as domestic companies are concerned, this applies both to direct insurance and reinsurance, whereas reinsurance business carried on by foreign concerns in Finland, is not supervised.

II. Adoption of the EC-acquis in Finland

When the EEA-agreement comes into force the Finnish Insurance legislation concerning insurance will be in line with the relevant acquis (*e.g.* with the second generation directives). In order to adapt the Finnish insurance legislation to the directives the Parliament has already passed three totally new bills and numerous amendment bills to the present insurance legislation. These bills will come into force at the same time as the EEA-agreement. Nevertheless, the Act abrogating the provisions of the Insurance Companies Act concerning foreign ownership and use of the right of decision by foreigners within insurance companies came into force 1.1.1993.

III. The regulations concerning the supervision of solvency

Due to the amended insurance company act, the Finnish insurance companies have to fulfil the requirements corresponding with the EC directives. The requirement of a plan for restoration and that of a short term financial scheme corresponding with the directives are also stated in the insurance company act. Besides, the insurance companies have to fulfil a risk theoretical solvency test which takes into account the special character of the company.

FRANCE

The need for policyholder protection, acknowledged in France as it is elsewhere, has prompted legislators and administrators to establish technical and financial rules. Reading through those rules undoubtedly provides the best possible initiation to the field of insurance.

The intended purpose of such regulations is to secure the long-term solvency of insurers, in order that they may always be in a position to honour their commitments.

Yet if regulatory requirements are analysed against the principles of sound management, they will be seen to represent only minimal precautions.

It is from this standpoint that the following principles and rules should be examined.

I.   Prudential rules

A.   *Pricing*

There are no particular provisions regarding non-life insurance.

For life insurance, the technical components of pricing are still subject to various restrictions (*e.g.* life tables, interest rates, underlying assets for unit-trust-linked contracts, etc.).

B.   *Technical reserves*

1. They must at all times be "sufficient to meet any liabilities to policyholders and beneficiaries".
2. They are calculated gross of claims and reinsurance ceded, and for each class of insurance.
3. For non-life insurance, premium reserves are generally prorated and equal no less than 36 per cent of premiums for unexpired risks. Claims reserves are calculated on a case-by-case basis or using statistical methods (frequency, average cost), and a management provision is added.
4. For life insurance, mathematical reserves are zillmerised.
   Theoretically, mathematical reserves are calculated on the same basis as premiums.

C. Assets representing technical reserves

- Liabilities, gross of reinsurance, must be represented by equivalent assets, generally located in France (except in the case of EC co-insurance and policies written under the freedom of service provision), expressed or realisable in the same currency as the underwriting liabilities.
- Liabilities must be represented by assets, and asset quality is regulated.
- In particular, and to give a simple description, such assets include: securities or comparable instruments issued or guaranteed by an OECD Member country or listed on an OECD-area stock exchange; shares in companies or in real property located in an OECD Member country; and loans obtained or guaranteed by natural or legal persons of OECD Member countries.
- Rules are imposed to limit and diversify assets. In particular, no more than 65 per cent of liabilities may be represented by shares, no more than 40 per cent by real estate assets and no more than 10 per cent by loans and deposits. The common diversification rule limits to 5 per cent the portion of liabilities that may be represented by securities issued by any one body (except for countries or the equivalent), and to 10 per cent the portion that may be represented by an investment in any one building.
- For life insurance, policy loans may be used to represent reserves.
- Claims on reinsurers may be used only if they are collateralised (*i.e.* if securities have been pledged).
- Assets are carried at their purchase price or at cost (with real assets depreciated).

No provision is made for unrealised capital losses on shares or real property unless the aggregate disposal value of these investments is below cost.

D. Capital

Depending upon the class of insurance, the minimum share capital required for licensing is either FF 5 million (for life, capitalisation, liability) or FF 3 million. At least half this amount must be contributed in cash at the time of incorporation.

The licensing authority may, however, require a far greater amount of initial capital, depending upon an insurer's projected premium volume.

The other prudential aspects related to capital are discussed in connection with the solvency margin.

E. Solvency ratios

The French method for assessing solvency is based on the concept of the solvency margin, which is taken from EC Directives of 1973 and 1979.

1. Non-life insurance

At the very least, the solvency margin must equal the greater of two ratios – one involving premiums due, gross of reinsurance but net of tax and cancellations (18 per cent, then 16 per cent); the other involving the average loss burden over the past three years (26 per cent, then 23 per cent) – adjusted by a post-reinsurance retention rate (*i.e.* the ratio of net claims to gross claims).

To determine whether a company covers its solvency margin, the following component elements are aggregated:

- paid-up share capital;
- half of non-paid-up share capital;
- supplementary contributions required of policyholders (in mutual insurance companies);
- subordinated debt;
- free reserves and retained earnings;
- capital gains arising from undervaluation of assets.

This method is applied on an aggregate basis to all classes of casualty insurance, gross of reinsurance accepted.

2. Life insurance

The minimum margin formula varies according to class and is based on ratios involving mathematical reserves gross of reinsurance, capital at risk or premiums due. The list of elements covering the margin is similar to the one for non-life insurance.

F. Supervision of insurance products

Contracts and prices are no longer subject to prior approval, but the Minister of the Economy and Finance can require insurers to submit contracts before they are distributed. The Minister then has one month in which to prescribe changes. If it is subsequently seen that a contract runs counter to regulations, the Minister may still require that it be withdrawn or amended.

G. Company officials and shareholders

Before an insurer can be licensed, it must submit a list of its directors and executive officers. In making a decision, the Minister considers the qualifications and experience of these officials, which must also be outlined in the licence application.

When the applicant is a limited liability company ("société anonyme"), the application must also contain a list of its principal shareholders.

General agents of branches of foreign insurers must, if they are legal persons, be domiciled or headquartered in France. The relevant professional experience requirements are identical to those applicable to officers of French companies.

The annual reports submitted to supervisory authorities also include updated information on members of the Board of Directors and executive personnel.

II. Supervision

A. Frequency of reporting and types of accounts furnished to supervisory authorities

Once a year, companies must provide the Insurance Supervisory Commission with two types of accounting and statistical documents:

- Public reports:
  - balance sheet, general operating account, profit and loss account, statement of earnings pending appropriation;
  - what are termed ''A'' reports, comprising chiefly general operating accounts by category and sub-category, a report on automobile premiums and claims, and a detailed list of investments.
- Reports prepared for the supervisory authority (''B'' reports), the most significant of which are B4 (assets representing regulated liabilities), B10 (payments and reserves for claims, by class and by year of occurrence) and B11 (solvency margin).

Companies must also provide the Insurance Supervisory Commission with quarterly reports on the investments representing their technical reserves.

B. On-site inspection

The Insurance Supervisory Commission delegates this task to insurance inspectors accredited to companies. The inspectors, who are technical officers with the Ministry of Finance, may extend their supervision to agencies and other intermediaries.

Inspectors exercise continuous supervision over insurers and make their own selections of the firms to be inspected on site, based on their experience with the companies and new information provided by annual reports.

C. Indicators

There are no standard indicators or set investigative procedures.

Such an approach is not only unnecessary, given the close, customised supervision, but inappropriate for the wide diversity of insurers (in terms of size, networks and legal status).

D. The importance of qualitative supervision

During their on-site examinations, inspectors may scrutinise various aspects of a company's operations and subsequently report any anomalies. The Insurance Supervisory Commission is empowered to suspend company officers temporarily if regulations have been violated.

The law clearly stipulates that the Supervisory Commission shall examine both the finances and the conditions of operation of insurance companies.

III. Measures taken in the event of problems

1. If it is found that a company's financial position has deteriorated, or that there has been a serious infringement of the regulations, the Insurance Supervisory Commission may either issue *a warning* or *enjoin the firm to take remedial measures* within a specified period of time.

If a company starts to act in a way that is contrary to the best interests of its policyholders (*e.g.* by offering severely deficient financial guarantees), the Insurance Supervisory Commission may require it to submit a short-term financial plan. If the Commission approves the plan, it is carried out by an insurance inspector invested with special supervisory powers. The Commission may also decide to freeze the company's assets.

The Commission may also exercise a number of restraining powers. In particular, it has a list of sanctions it may use to bring a firm found wanting back to normal operation or to discontinue any activity that has gone counter to policyholders' best interests. These sanctions are: warnings, reprimands, the prohibition of certain transactions and any other limitation of operations, temporary suspension of one or more company company officers, total or partial withdrawal of licensing, and compulsory transfer of portfolio.

2. Liquidation

A firm is liquidated after the Insurance Supervisory Commission withdraws its licence. The liquidator proceeds under judicial authority and is assisted by insurance inspectors. Non-life policies cease to attach 40 days after a licence is withdrawn; for life insurance, the ultimate solution depends upon the liquidator's assessment of the situation and may consist of a portfolio transfer, payment deferments, reduction of indemnities, etc.

The liquidator disposes of assets and indemnifies creditors in the order of priority established by law:

The order of priority of claims is:

- sums due to employees;
- liquidator's expenses;
- sums due to the State and to labour organisations;
- sums due to policyholders and beneficiaries; first to settle claims, then to reimburse excess premium payments.

If assets are insufficient, the proceeds are distributed pro rata among creditors having equal priority of claims. The liquidator is empowered to come to terms with holders of doubtful claims.

3. International issues

Foreign companies doing business in France are liquidated according to the above procedure, on the basis of a special analysis of French operations.

No special treatment is reserved for foreign policyholders, whose position cannot be more favourable than that of domestic customers.

IV. Special issues relating to groups of insurers

Such issues are currently under discussion on a European level. No decision on separate procedures for the supervision of multi-company groups should be made until Brussels has taken a stance on the issue.

V.   Special issues relating to reinsurance

The technical reserves of ceding companies are calculated gross of reinsurance. The assets representing these regulated liabilities may include claims on reinsurers, provided those claims are guaranteed by securities pledged to the cedent. The insolvency of reinsurers (which, in France, are not subject to State supervision) is therefore not a problem, so long as the rule that technical reserves be covered gross is complied with.

VI. Separation between life and non-life

In France, companies may not conduct both types of business at the same time.

As a result, current regulations distinguish, when necessary, between the two areas and generally make separate provisions for each.

VII. Special issues relating to specific types of insurance products

-   In the case of unit-trust-linked life insurance, mathematical reserves are represented by investments in the securities that make up the reference unit, in the same proportions.
-   There are special provisions governing certain contracts for which a higher-than-normal rate is allowed in setting premiums and calculating mathematical reserves. In such cases (*e.g.* single-premium capitalisation contracts with a maximum maturity of 15 years), the corresponding asset must be kept separate and generate returns that are at least one percentage point greater than the rate used to calculate mathematical reserves.

VIII. Adapting the current system to recent economic trends

The French regulatory framework is about to change, in connection with European Directives. Among the areas involved will be the liquidation of failed businesses, pension funds and financial conglomerates – all of which are being affected by the structural changes currently under way in the EC economies.

GERMANY

I. Financial supervision

A. *Legal bases of financial supervision*

Financial supervision of insurance companies is mainly based on the provisions of the Law on the Supervision of Insurance Companies (Insurance Supervision Law), the Commercial Code, the Stock Corporation Law, and the Regulations on External and Internal Accounting. While both the Civil Code and Stock Corporation Law contain provisions applicable also to non-insurance companies, the Insurance Supervision Law and the two Regulations apply only to insurance companies.

B. *Actual organisation of financial supervision*

1. *Organisation of the insurance supervisory authority*

The duties of financial supervision are mainly performed by two out of a total of seven divisions of the Federal Insurance Supervisory Office. One division deals with matters concerning non-life insurance – excluding health insurance – (which comes under the specialisation requirement in Germany) and reinsurance. The other division deals with matters concerning financial supervision of life and health insurances; moreover, general questions concerning investments of life and non-life insurance companies come within its competence. At present the number of employees in both divisions are 33 and 39 respectively. Each division comprises six sections each consisting of section head and one to three civil servants. As regards their professional qualification most of them are holders of a diploma in business administration.

2. *Areas coming under financial supervision*

Financial supervision begins with the procedure for the authorisation of an insurance company to carry on insurance business. During this procedure particular attention is given to adequate own funds and the establishment of an organisation fund. In addition, the insurance companies have to submit estimations of commission expenses, other current operating expenses, expected premiums, expected claims expenses and expected liquidity position in the first three years. The applicable provisions of the German insurance supervision legislation are mainly based on the harmonised conditions for the authorisation to take up insurance business including the provision of insurance companies with own funds of EC Directives 73/239/EC (First Non-Life Directive) and 79/267/EC (First Life Directive) which have been enacted into national law, as amended by the third Directive 92/49/EC or 92/96/EC.

After authorisation the business operations of insurance companies are subject to on-going supervision. Information about the financial situation of insurance companies are mainly obtained from the externally published annual accounts, the records to be submitted according to the Regulation on internal accounting, statistical surveys, and on-site inspections of insurance companies.

The essentials of on-going supervision are:

– *Solvency control*
According to Section 53c (1), first sentence of the Insurance Supervision Law the insurance companies are required, for the purpose of securing their ability to meet their liabilities under insurance policies at any time, to establish free and uncommitted own funds in an amount not less than the solvency margin which depends on the volume of business. The calculation method and the amount of the required own funds have been stipulated in the Regulation on the funding of insurance companies. The rules concerning the submission of the external annual accounts and internal accounting documents to the insurance supervisory authority have been adapted to the third directives and Directive 91/674/EC (directive on the annual accounts of insurance companies). In particular as far as reporting to the supervisory authority is concerned, new statements covering the insurance business written in the EC member States were necessary to meet the reporting requirements of the third directives. The above provisions are mainly based on the harmonised solvency requirements according to EC Directives 73/239/EC and 79/267/EC which have been enacted into national law.

– *Control of insurance companies' investments*
The insurance companies may within the framework of the provisions of the Insurance Supervision Law take their own investment decisions. The investments of insurance companies are not subject to prior approval by the insurance supervisory authority; this does not apply to the exemptions which the insurance supervisory authority may grant, for instance, with regard to types of investment not mentioned in the Insurance Supervision Law or if certain limits are exceeded. The investment rules do not require the insurance companies to invest in certain types of investments. Therefore, the third directives only stipulate certain limits for the types of investments to ensure their safety. Even if the German legislator wished to favour investments in certain areas he would not be permitted to require the insurance companies to comply with this wish. As regards investments the insurance companies are required to submit to the insurance supervisory authority a number of (subsequent) notifications in particular also concerning certain new investments.

– *General analysis of annual accounts*
This mainly concentrates on the technical reserves on the liabilities side of the balance sheet. In non-life insurance in particular the adequate allocation of funds

to the provisions for outstanding claims is supervised; since estimations are used to establish these provisions a certain margin is left as regards fixing the required amount of these provisions. In life insurance the main emphasis is on the control of the mathematical reserves which are calculated on actuarial principles.

Financial supervision of day-to-day business is to ensure that the insurance companies are in a position to meet their liabilities under the insurance contracts at any time.

II. Measures to be taken in case of financial difficulties of insurance companies

If the amount of an insurance company's own funds is less than the solvency margin the company shall, on request of the supervisory authority, submit for approval a plan to restore sound financial conditions (solvency plan) [Section 81*b* (1) of the Insurance Supervision Law]. If an insurance company's own funds are less than the guarantee fund the company shall, on request of the supervisory authority, submit for approval a plan for the short-term procurement of the necessary own funds (financing plan) [Section 81*b* (2), first sentence of the Insurance Supervision Law]. Moreover, the insurance supervisory authority may limit or prohibit free disposition of the assets of the company [Section 81*b* (2), second sentence of the Insurance Supervision Law].

As regards investments the insurance supervisory authority may prohibit an insurance company from continuing to hold a participation in another company which is not supervised, if any such participation is, by its nature or scope, likely to endanger the insurance company [Section 82 (1), of the Insurance Supervision Law].

If the technical reserves of an insurance company are not adequately represented by qualifying investment the insurance supervisory authority may limit or prohibit free disposition of the assets of the company [Section 81*b* (4), of the Insurance Supervision Law]. The same applies if an insurance company does not establish adequate technical reserves.

The Insurance Supervision Law contains additional rules permitting the insurance supervisory authority to interfere in certain specific cases. Under certain conditions it is entitled to appoint a special commissioner [Section 81 (2*a*), of the Insurance Supervision Law] and to transfer to him all rights which the company bodies dispose of by law or under the articles of association, to withdraw the authorisation to do business either fully or partly in very severe cases [Section 87, of the Insurance Supervision Law] and to require changes to be made in existing contracts [Section 89 of the Insurance Supervision Law]. In case of withdrawal of the authorisation the insurance supervisory authority may take all suitable measures to safeguard the interests of the insured, in particular limit or prohibit free disposition of the assets of the company and entrust qualified persons with the management of the assets [Section 87 (4), of the Insurance Supervision Law].

Moreover, the insurance supervisory authority may give the necessary orders to ensure compliance of business operations with the legal requirements and operating plan or to remove irregularities which endanger the interests of the insured or cause business operations to be in conflict with good practice [Section 81 (2), first sentence of the Insurance Supervision Law].

To avoid serious interference with a company's freedom to take decisions, as mentioned above, attempts are being made within the framework of on-going supervision to prevent any situations which would require such measures to be taken beforehand.

To prevent any restoration measures to be endangered by third parties (such as creditors of the insurance company), only the insurance supervisory authority is entitled to file a petition in bankruptcy [Section 88 (1), of the Insurance Supervision Law]. In case of insolvency or overindebtedness the board of directors of an insurance company shall inform the insurance supervisory authority accordingly which will examine whether bankruptcy can be avoided in the interest of the policyholders and take the necessary action (Section 89 of the Insurance Supervision Law). All kinds of payments, especially of benefits, participations in profits and, in the case of life insurance, surrender values or policy loans and advances on policies may be temporarily prohibited [Section 89 (1), second sentence of the Insurance Supervision Law]. Under certain conditions the insurance supervisory authority may reduce the liabilities of a life insurance company under its insurance policies [Section 89 (2), first sentence of the Insurance Supervision Law].

GREECE

I. Regulation concerning the supervision of solvency

Each insurance undertaking is obliged to set up a solvency margin in respect of its entire business corresponding to its assets free of its entire business corresponding to its assets free of foreseeable, less any intangible items.

Also each insurance undertaking must set up a guarantee fund. The guarantee fund must represent one third of the solvency margin.

The Ministry of Commerce, in order to ascertain the observance by the insurance undertakings of the provisions of the law concerning the solvency margin and the guarantee fund, must carry out a control of their financial situation at least once a year.

For the Class 18 (assistance) the control also deals with the qualifications of the staff, as well as with the quality of the equipment disposed by the undertakings in order to meet the obligations imposed by this class. The said control is carried out in close collaboration with the competent Services of the relevant Ministries.

Every insurance undertaking, during its first three financial years, is obliged to submit to the Ministry of Commerce, every six months the particulars provided by Article 19 of the Law 2170/93 with a view to cross check its financial position in relation to the submitted scheme of operations.

According to the above mentioned Article 19:

– Every insurance undertaking submits to the Ministry for Commerce, annually and within two months from the publication of its Balance Sheet, a summary relating to the previous year consisting of:
  • A statement indicating the number of concluding contracts per class of insurance and the number and total amounts of indemnities paid and outstanding and of the unexpired risks.
  • A statement showing per class of insurance the total amount of premiums written and collected.
– The Life Insurance Undertakings additionally submit:
  A statement showing the total amount of concluded contracts per class of insurance, the amount of loans granted to assured, the amount of insurance paid and cancelled, the amount of insurances and validity, the amount of insurances trans-

ferred from abroad to Greece and of insurance transferred from Greece abroad due to the corresponding change of the assured residence.

- A summary of the data stated in the above mentioned is published in the Bulletin of Insurance.
- A decision of the Ministry for Commerce to determine a standard form for the submission of the above data, relating to the annual business of the insurance undertakings. In the case of Greek and foreign insurance undertakings already operating, the pledging of assets allocated in insurance investment may be lifted by resolution of the Minister for Commerce on the application of the insurance undertaking, accompanied by supporting documents proving that the undertaking possesses the solvency margin and the guarantee fund in compliance with Articles 17a and 17b (calculations for solvency margin) of the Law 400/1970.

II. The practical organisation of the supervision

The competent authority for the supervision of the solvency of the insurance undertakings is the Directorate of Insurance, in the Ministry for Commerce.

The supervising authorities exerce their control through the above mentioned submitted once a year standard from of all data relating to the annual business of the insurance undertakings.

Also, in order to verify compliance with the financial rules applicable, the supervising authorities may carry out an on-the-spot investigation when this appears appropriate.

Furthermore, the supervising authorities exchange information and collaborate permanently with other supervisory authorities such as banks.

III. Measures when difficulties arise (recovery measures)

Should the solvency margin possessed by the insurance undertaking fall below the minimum amount required, it must submit to the Ministry for Commerce a plan for the restoration of a sound financial position for approval.

Should the actual solvency margin also fall below the guarantee fund that the insurance undertaking must possess or if the guarantee fund is not constituted in compliance with the relative provisions, the insurance undertakings must submit to the Ministry for Commerce a short-term finance scheme.

Pending such completion, the Minister for Commerce may prohibit the free disposal of all or part of the assets of the insurance undertaking and take all measures necessary to safeguard the policyholders' interests.

The Minister for Commerce may withdraw the licence for all classes operated by the insurance undertaking if it fails to comply within the time limit allowed, within the measures contained in the restoration plan or finance scheme in accordance with the above mentioned.

ICELAND

The insurance business in Iceland is regulated by Law No. 50/1978 on Insurance Activity. In this law and Regulation No. 482/1981 the rules and measures concerning supervision of solvency of insurance companies are laid down. The Act No. 50/1978 applies to any kind of insurance activity operated on commercial basis, both direct and indirect insurance. The insurance companies are not allowed to carry on any other business than insurance business or business directly connected with that, and cannot own subsidiaries which are not insurance companies. There are 25 companies operating in the country of which four have about 80 per cent of premium volume for own account.

A fundamental provision of the law is that the Insurance Supervisory Authority has the right at any time to claim any documents and information from the company and to do any on-the-spot investigations they like and find necessary to be able to fulfil their obligations as supervisors, one of the main objects of the supervision being to secure the solvency of insurance companies licensed to operate in the country.

I. Regulations concerning the supervision of insurance solvency

A. *The solvency margin*

Upon establishment of a domestic limited insurance company the share capital shall amount to a minimum of 30-35 million IKr. A mutual insurance company shall have guarantee capital amounting to a minimum of 20-25 million IKr. A foreign insurance company carrying on insurance business in Iceland shall submit evidence to the effect that its assets in the country amount to not less than 15-20 million IKr and the company shall prove annually that its assets in Iceland come to such an amount.

The solvency margin of domestic and foreign insurance companies being licensed to engage in insurance activity in Iceland shall come to a minimum of the aforementioned amounts at each given time.

The solvency margin, as defined below, shall however at each time amount to at least the minimum solvency margin specified by the higher of two amounts computed in accordance with the following:

- 18 per cent of the gross premium income after deductions of refunds and cancellations but without deducting reinsurer's part of premiums multiplied by the ratio between paid claims for own account and paid claims totally. In case this ratio be lower than 0.35 multiplication shall occur by 0.35.

- 13 per cent of the amount obtained upon adding up paid claims during the last two fiscal years without deducting reinsurer's part plus the claims reserve at the end of the latest fiscal year, but deducting the claims reserve in the beginning of the first fiscal year. The quantity thus obtained is multiplied by the ratio in 1 or by the figure 0.35 if the latter is higher.

The minimum solvency margin of life insurance companies shall however be computed solely according to I. hereinbefore for life insurance business with no savings part.

The solvency margin of an insurance company is that amount which is obtained when any kind of liabilities, immaterial assets and depreciations have been deducted from the company's total assets. In this connection the following items are included in the solvency margin:

- paid-up share capital or guarantee capital after deducting own share capital;
- half the unpaid capital provided that paid-up capital amounts to a least 25 per cent of the total;
- legal reserve funds or other funds which according to the by-laws of the company are intended to meet deficit and are not liabilities of any kind;
- the company's investment risk reserve;
- profit brought forward from previous years;
- hidden reserves when assets are valued lower than real value in the balance sheet or liabilities are counted too high, provided that the hidden reserves are considered not to be occasional. Hidden reserves being part of the technical provisions may be included up to 75 per cent in non-life companies but as estimated by the actuary in life companies. The amount under this item must not exceed 50 per cent of the solvency margin as a whole.

Upon calculating the solvency margin in accordance with the foregoing, insecure assets shall not be included. Reduction of items of assets shall be computed to the extent which is deemed necessary and the reduction of the following items of assets shall never be less than:

- 7.5 per cent of premiums outstanding;
- 5.0 per cent of debts of agents and of other domestic debtors;
- 3.5 per cent of bills of exchange held;
- 1.0 per cent of domestic bonds and interest fallen due with exception of those being guaranteed by the State.

B. The technical provisions

An insurance company shall contribute part of its profit each year to an equalisation reserve. It may only be used to meet deficit due to adverse development of loss payments during any year, and only after receipt of permission by the Minister and recommendation of the Supervision. Apart from this, the Insurance Act or Regulations do not stipulate rules or system for the size of the technical provisions of non-life insurance companies or how to fix a sufficient amount to set aside. There are only general formulations in the law on the necessity and duty of the company to provide for sufficient technical provisions so that the company can meet its commitments due to the insurance contracts. The technical provisions shall include provisions for unsettled claims, reported and not yet reported, and safety surcharge sufficient to take care of random and systematic fluctuations.

A life insurance company however must furnish an actuarial basis for the technical provisions and it is not permitted to alter this basis except with the permission of the Minister of Insurance Affairs after having obtained recommendation of the Insurance Supervisory Authority.

Only in respect of life insurance does the Insurance Act prescribe matching rules of assets equal to the technical provisions. The life insurance fund must be invested in certain kinds of assets such as in banks, governmental bonds, loans secured by mortgage on real estate up to 60 per cent of value, in real estate owned by the company up to 60 per cent of value, etc.

C. The reinsurance coverage

In the Insurance Act rules for the maximum risk an insurance company is allowed to bear in any one loss incident for own account are given. A formula is based on the solvency margin, safety loadings of the premiums and overall risk as estimated by the losses incurred in one year for own account. This is a thumb rule based on approximations and relying on risk theoretical considerations. The formula for the maximum risk H is as follows:

$$H = 0.16 \times T \times (G/T + A)^2, \text{ but never exceeding } 0.08 \times G$$

where G represents the solvency margin of the company, T losses incurred for own account during the year according to the Profit and Loss Account, and A is a jointly weighed assessment of the safety loadings of the premiums. In case a company's own risk be, in the judgement of the Insurance Supervisory Authority, higher than the maximum risk when regard has been had for an accumulation effect, the company shall make arrangements before the end of the fiscal year, or as soon as possible, regarding reinsurance contracts in force, in order to bring its reinsurance protection in line with the stipulated rules.

D. The premium level

The premium level is in all branches of life and non-life insurance, subject to control of the Insurance Supervision according to the Insurance Act and it is in fact control on beforehand. The premium tables shall be sent to the Supervision before use. The premium level shall, according to the law, correspond to the risk involved and the risk premiums shall be loaded with a cost factor which is ''reasonable''. The premiums shall be ''fair'', not too low so that the company cannot meet its commitments, and not too high so that the customers pay unreasonable price for their insurance protection.

A life insurance company must submit to the Insurance Supervisory Authority a technical basis for approval giving exact rules for, among other things, the computation of premiums, bonus payments, surrender values and paid-up policies.

E. The investments

The Insurance Act does not include any special provisions or conditions regarding the investment policy of the companies, nor does it prescribe exact rules for the composition or spread of the assets, except as mentioned earlier, in life insurance where detailed rules are given regarding the kinds of assets allowed to match against the technical provisions.

F. Management costs

The Insurance Act does not have any provisions on management costs except the one mentioned earlier, *i.e.* the general statement about the loadings for management costs and the corresponding component in the premiums offered, which shall be within reasonable limits.

It should be mentioned that the Law No. 50 on Insurance Activity which dates back to 1978 is under revision and a proposal on a new bill will probably be adopted in the autumn 1993 or in the spring 1994. This proposal includes adaption to the EC-legislation and the European Economic Area which with certainty will result in changes of the present legislation in various respects.

II. The practical organisation of supervision of solvency

The supervision of solvency is carried out by collecting detailed data from the companies usually on a yearly basis, and by on-the-spot investigations with the companies. The latter can include certain areas or specific cases only, but it can also be a question of investigating the company as a whole. There may be special reason for the investigation, it can also be a part of the routine to visit each company regularly.

The companies must fill in several forms as prescribed by the Insurance Supervision, among them one on specification of the solvency margin of the company and send to the Supervision yearly together with the annual accounts and the Supervision makes calculations and comparisons with the minimum solvency margin. Another form filled in and sent to the Supervision concerns the technical provisions. Detailed data on the run-off of the claims reserves in each branch of insurance in non-life business are yearly sent to the Supervision separated on accounting years and loss years. The development is studied within each company and a judgement made whether the claims reserves can be considered as adequate. Among the methods used are chain-ladder methods to get an idea of the strength of the claims reserves. Another method used considers distributions of the time lag of the run-off, which varies considerably between branches. A special problem has been to decide whether hidden reserves can be considered as included in the technical reserves, which may be included in the solvency margin. Also information is given on special form regarding the reinsurance coverage in the various branches and the companies are bound to report to the Supervision the main features of the reinsurance contracts, type, limits and largest losses in each branch so that comparisons can be made with the maximum risk formula as mentioned earlier.

The premium level is controlled by analysing the loss development as compared with the premiums paid in each branch and comparing loss ratios between years and branches. Detailed information is also given on forms by each company on every item of assets and liabilities in the Balance Sheet, and this information is the basis for the assessment of the financial risk involved in the investments of the company and judgement of spread and composition of the portfolio, which is especially considered in connection with calculations of the solvency margin. Detailed data are also collected on the main items of the management costs of each company.

III. Measures when difficulties arise (recovery measures)

In the case the solvency margin of an insurance company does not reach the minimum limits according to the annual computation, the company shall according to the law make immediate arrangements so that the limit may be reached within a specific respite. That respite should not be longer than six months if the solvency margin is lower than one third of the minimum. In case it becomes clear to an insurance company at another time that its solvency margin does not meet the minimum limit, the company shall likewise make arrangements for the limit to be reached.

The company shall within two months give the Insurance Supervision an account in writing about the arrangements it intends to make and how the limit will be reached.

The Insurance Supervision shall also assess the liquidity of an insurance company on the basis of the annual account or at another time if there is deemed to be reason therefore. In case the liquidity is considered as unsatisfactory the Supervision shall give the company notice of the conclusions and the company shall forthwith make the requisite arrangements for amends.

In case the insurance company does not heed a request from the Supervision relating to amendments to terms or premiums or violates laws or Regulations respecting insurance activity or the solvency margin is too low, the Supervision shall forthwith advise the Minister of the matter and submit proposals as to what should be done. The Minister shall give the company suitable respite to make amends. In case the company has not effected the requisite improvements within a specific respite the Minister may withdraw the company's licence. In case the Minister withdraws a licence he shall appoint three members to the company's administration board. That board will take over the entire authority of the company's board of directors when authority of the latter will simultaneously be cancelled. The administration board shall forthwith convene a company meeting and acquaint shareholders/owners with the situation which has developed. The board shall render a decision as to whether bankruptcy administration shall be requested or whether it shall continue to be operated for a time and business shall be completed without bankruptcy administration. In assessing what shall be done the main regard shall be had for the interests of the insured.

If it is a life insurance company the administration board shall forthwith take assets of the life insurance fund into custody and the Insurance Supervisory Authority shall within six months apply for other life companies to take over the life insurance portfolio and the life insurance fund.

The Supervision shall assess the offers submitted, selecting the one they deem most favourable for the insured. After having received comments the Minister may convey to the company selected by the Supervision, the life insurance portfolio and the assets of the life insurance fund. In case no offer be received for the take-over or the Supervision cannot recommend any, the life fund shall be paid out to the insured in correct proportion to the value of their life insurance in the fund.

No other measures are given in the law text, or alternatives for recoveries of the situation. In practice however, when an adverse situation is observed, and before it comes to the procedure described by the law, the Supervision and the company have bilateral contacts. The company is requested to make appropriate amendments of the situation, if necessary to present a restoration plan, in close co-operation with the Supervision, the Ministry being kept informed. Iceland got a special legislation in this field as late as 1973. No forced winding-up of direct insurance companies has occurred the 20 years that have passed since then, and recovery of the situation has been possible in several cases, some of them being rather serious ones in this period.

IRELAND

I. Regulations governing the supervision of solvency

The basic objective of financial supervision of insurance companies in Ireland is that of ensuring that insurers firstly, maintain sufficient assets to cover their liabilities to policyholders and secondly, meet the minimum solvency margin requirements specified in the EC Directives. In order to achieve this, insurers are required effectively to maintain solvency at three levels in the following descending order.

A. *Underwriting liabilities and equivalent assets*

The most basic layer of solvency of an insurer is the ability to cover its policyholder liabilities with equivalent and matching assets. Matching in this sense means that the assets backing the underwriting liabilities should be denominated in the currency of the underwriting liabilities. The amount of the reserves required to meet these policyholder liabilities is determined, in general, by the State where the undertaking carries on business. Another important feature is the necessity for an insurer to hold assets backing policyholder liabilities in categories which are approved categories. There are also rules which determine the maximum levels of policyholder liabilities which certain assets can represent. In this context, insurers must exercise care that they achieve the necessary spread of assets.

In the context of EC insurance undertakings, the third generation directives due to come into effect in July 1994 while they do not harmonise Member States regulations in relation to the nature, spread and valuation of assets representing the insurance liabilities do lay down rules which:

- confine the list of acceptable assets to certain categories;
- specify the maximum amount of insurance liabilities certain assets may represent; and
- set out the guiding principles to be followed in the valuation of assets.

The mutual recognition is very important in the context of the third generation EC Directives where the establishment of reserves will be solely under the control of the home Member State. (The "home Member State" is the Community State in which the insurance undertaking's head office is located.)

The assets acceptable as cover for the liabilities include shares, debt securities, bonds, bank deposits and property.

B.   *Minimum guarantee fund*

The intermediate layer of solvency required of insurers is the minimum guarantee fund which, subject to certain minimum limits, is equivalent to one third of the solvency margin. The minimum guarantee fund for non-life insurance business is ECU 200 000 where as, for life insurance it is ECU 800 000.

C.   *Solvency margin*

The final and ultimate measurement of an insurance company's financial health is the requirement that it maintain a solvency margin which, in effect is an excess of free assets over liabilities. The minimum margins of solvency are calculated differently for life and non-life business. For non-life insurers, the method of calculation of the solvency margin is set down in Article 16 of the First Non-Life Directive (73/239/EC).

There are two methods of calculation – the Premiums and Claims Basis. The Premiums Basis is calculated by reference to the volume of gross premiums written in a financial year while the Claims Basis is calculated by reference to the average burden of incurred claims over a three-year period. The solvency margin to be maintained is the higher of the two calculations. The minimum margin on the premiums basis is 16 per cent of gross annual premium income or, if greater, 23 per cent of the annual claims.

For life business, the method of calculation is set down in the First Life Directive No. 79/267/EC. The minimum solvency margin requirement for life business is equivalent to between 0.1 per cent and 0.3 per cent of capital at risk.

II.   The practical organisation of supervision

The Supervisory Authority requires each authorised insurance company to file audited financial returns on an annual basis. For newly authorised companies inaudited accounts are required at more frequent intervals (*i.e.* quarterly or biannually) for at least the first three years of operation. The type of accounts which are required include a Revenue account which provides information on the levels of premium written; cost of claims; commission levels and, in the case of non-life the underwriting result for each class of business. Balance Sheet, Profit and Loss account, asset valuation form and statement of solvency margin are also required.

Upon receipt of the accounts, the Supervisory Authority examines in detail the set of accounts presented with particular regard to the level of reserves set up, the cost of claims and the level of management expenses. These analyses provide the basic indicators from which decisions can be taken on the need for follow-up for instance on inadequate reserves or reserving methodology with the company concerned. Having examined the adequacy of the reserves required by a company, the nature and acceptability of the assets put forward to meet these liabilities are then examined. The basis of this examination is to see that the range of assets included are soundly based and that their spread is sufficiently prudent in the light of the claims likely to be made on the insurer.

The second level in the supervisory mechanism relates to the solvency margin requirement. The solvency margin is calculated by reference to the company's total business wherever this is conducted. Under EC Directives, responsibility for the verification of the solvency margin rests with the supervisory authority in whose territory the Head Office is located. Having identified the level of solvency margin to be established, the Supervisory Authority then examines the adequacy and acceptability of the assets available to the company to meet this requirement. This can be monitored both by analysing the movement of assets and liabilities within the Balance Sheet and Profit and Loss Account and also through the use of asset analysis returns whereby it is possible to establish the appropriate value of total assets held and then to match these assets to the technical reserve requirement, the current liabilities and the solvency margin requirement itself.

III. Recovery measures

Failure to maintain the required solvency margin results in an undertaking being required to submit a plan for the restoration of a sound financial position to the supervisory authority of the Head Office for approval. If the solvency margin falls below the level of the minimum Guarantee Fund (defined as being equal to one-third of the solvency margin) an undertaking is required to submit a short-term finance scheme for approval. Failure to restore the solvency margin within the time allowed may result in an undertaking's authorisation being withdrawn.

The Supervisory Authority also has powers under the 1989 Insurance Act to intervene in cases of doubtful solvency. The powers vested in the Supervisory Authority include a right to give a direction to an insurer to refrain from taking on new business; to limit premium income to a set amount; to refrain from making investments in specified timeframe; to maintain in the state assets of a value equal to the whole or a specified amount of its liabilities in the State.

ITALY

ISVAP, the Italian insurance industry regulator, was set up by the 1982 Act which amended the system of insurance supervision. Its role is to:

- oversee the technical, financial and asset management of insurance and reinsurance companies;
- analyse companies' balance sheets;
- ensure compliance (by agents, insurance and reinsurance brokers) with insurance laws and regulations.

The following functions of the ISVAP are particularly important:

- monitoring the international and Community insurance market;
- studying trends in risks, risk prevention and cover;
- determining the elements on the basis of which rates are calculated and checked, and policy terms are examined.

ISVAP also issues opinions on the business plans submitted by companies when they apply for a licence, and on recovery and financial plans. It can propose to the Ministry of Industry that statutory sanctions be taken against a company, including withdrawal of its licence and compulsory liquidation. It promotes collaboration with other EU insurance supervisory authorities with a view to harmonising the supervision of freely-supplied insurance activities. The measures taken to ensure the solvency of insurers are summarised below.

I. Regulations concerning the supervision of solvency

A. *Authorisation to engage in insurance activities, and to engage in other classes of insurance business*

Before issuing a licence, ISVAP takes into account the administrative, accounting and technical aspects of a company's situation.

More specifically, the authorised capital of life insurance companies may not be less than ten times the minimum prescribed capital for joint-stock companies. In practice, depending on the company's organisation and volume of business, the total capital required (authorised capital and organisation fund) may not be less than L 15 billion.

The following are also examined: the company's instrument of incorporation and statutes, the list of directors, legal representatives and general managers, the business plan, the undertaking on the part of the company to report to ISVAP any changes it plans to make, during the first five years of activity, in its statutes, directors, legal representatives and general management; it also examines the system of internal controls.

Lastly, ISVAP may require the majority shareholder not to transfer its controlling interest during the first three years of activity.

Companies that apply for a non-life licence must have a minimum authorised capital, the amount of which varies according to the class of business, and an adequate organisation fund.

In particular, companies applying for a licence to sell third-party motor insurance must have a minimum authorised capital of L 2 billion. In practice, the average minimum capital required (authorised capital and organisation fund), especially for companies that do not belong to an insurance group, is L 10 million when the volume of premium income is large.

Directors, legal representatives and general managers must prove that they are fit to carry out their duties.

The business plan is looked at very closely. It must mention the risks that the company intends to cover, reinsurance criteria, the assets that constitute the authorised capital, estimates of start-up costs, overheads, premium income and outgoing on losses, and estimates of the financial resources required to meet the solvency margin.

The documentation must be accompanied by a technical annex setting out the criteria used in drawing up the business plan.

If a company wishes to write other classes of insurance business, ISVAP examines its business plan and checks that the solvency margin and technical provision requirements continue to be complied with.

B. Rates and policy terms

To obtain a licence, or to have its licence extended to other classes of insurance, a company must attach to its business plan (except for special classes) its general and special policy terms, and the rates it plans to charge for each type of business.

C. Solvency margin

As required by the regulations, ISVAP looks particularly closely at the solvency margin, taking into account any rectifications to the valuation of assets (capital losses) and technical liabilities (inadequate technical provisions).

If the minimum solvency margin is not met, the company is requested to draw up a recovery plan or, if the available solvency margin is less than the minimum guarantee fund, to submit a short-term finance scheme which must indicate the measures the company intends to take it to restore its asset base.

If the solvency margin is less than the minimum guarantee fund, the company may be forbidden to dispose of assets located in Italy, and the competent authorities of other EU countries in which the company operates must be informed accordingly.

These authorities may also be requested to take similar steps in respect of assets which the company has on their territory. An order is issued to mortgage the company's real estate assets; the securities and cash deposits constituting its technical provisions are also placed in deposit and mortgaged. Similar steps are taken if a company is banned from writing new business because it has violated the rules on technical provisions, or before completion of consultations with the competent supervisory authorities in other EU countries in which the company operates.

D. Technical provisions

ISVAP takes particular care to check that companies have valued their technical provisions correctly and that they have sufficient assets to cover them, and that the breakdown of the different assets complies with the regulations.

It does this by means of on-the-spot inspections or statistical methods.

When ISVAP carries out on-the-spot investigations, it frequently puts on diskette the data regarding the amounts set aside for reserves and payments. It can thus check that the provisions are adequate.

As regards the different types of assets that can be used to cover technical provisions, both real estate and securities are allowed, as well as specific types of deposits, loans and other special categories of credit.

If a company does not meet the requirements regarding technical provisions, it is invited to comply with them, and may also be forbidden to dispose of its assets in Italy. The competent authorities of the other EU countries in which the company operates must be notified of this. Lastly, if the company fails to complies with the recommendations of ISVAP, it can be banned from writing new business.

E. Balance sheet analysis

Analysis of the balance sheets which are returned annually by insurance companies is another important aspect of supervision. A set of indicators was compiled for this purpose. After they have been processed automatically, these indicators make it possible to appraise a company's situation rapidly and objectively.

The balance sheet analysis provides a basis for any further investigations by inspectors. Auditors' and actuaries' reports are also used. They serve as a framework for the assessment of the company's situation and its assets.

F. Early warning indicators

It proved necessary to devise criteria and methods for identifying in good time those insurance companies that have got into difficulty, so as to be able to avert a collapse. Such indicators were particularly needed for third- party motor insurance, a sector of considerable importance in the Italian market.

Several balance sheet indicators were considered; of these, 18 relating to technical characteristics and assets were selected. The limits within which these indicators could fluctuate were defined, and companies were then classified according to the number of indicators that fell outside this range.

These indicators, for non-life insurance, are listed below:
- Trading result/premiums.
- Solvency margin.
- Ordinary profits.
- Extraordinary profits.
- Liquidity/technical provisions for direct insurance.
- Holdings/total assets.
- Other assets/total assets.

Third-party motor insurance
- Result for this class of business/premiums.
- Cost of claims.
- Cost of claims for current year.
- Cost of previous claims arising from the inadequacy of provisions.
- Ordinary profits.
- Extraordinary profits.
- Loading/premiums.
- Motor vehicle premiums/total premiums.
- Reserve for outstanding claims/premiums.
- Speed with which claims during current year were settled (number).
- Speed with which claims during previous years were settled (number).

Given that annual balance sheet data are out-of-date by the time they are received, an intra-annual information system based on variables that are the most significant for an insurance company's management is being designed, with a view to ensuring effective supervision of the entire insurance sector.

II. Practical organisation of supervision

On-the-spot inspections are also very important, and are necessary when ISVAP cannot carry out checks directly. The following are usually checked:
- that the accounts and valuations of insurance and reinsurance activities are correct;
- general compliance with insurance regulations;
- the reliability of internal procedures.

III. Measures when difficulties arise

A. *Supervision of shareholdings, acquisitions, and intragroup transactions*

Specific supervision of shareholdings, acquisitions, and transactions involving transfers of assets between companies belonging to the same group was recently introduced with a view to preventing any reduction in the asset base of insurance companies arising from other activities of the controlling group. Groups are also required to draw up a consolidated balance sheet.

B. *Administrative measures*

For the least serious irregularities, *i.e.* those that can be resolved without it being necessary to appoint outside administrators, ISVAP can convene a meeting of shareholders, the board of directors, or any other organ of management.

In the case of a serious breach of the regulations or serious administrative irregularities, the action that can be taken range from the appointment of an officer to dissolve the company's management or board of auditors, to the appointment of one or more special administrators. If irregularities have taken place or the law has been infringed, financianl penalties can also be imposed.

As already mentioned, recovery or short-term finance schemes are very important.

If the company fails to allow access to inspectors or commits a serious breach of insurance law and regulations, its licence can be withdrawn, thereby triggering the compulsory liquidation procedure.

C. *Guarantee fund for road casualties*

A guarantee fund for road casualties has been set up to cover claims arising from accidents caused by unidentified vehicles, vehicles that were not insured or were insured by companies that were being wound up when the accident occurred.

The fund is financed by contributions from companies that supply motor insurance, calculated as a percentage of the premiums collected for this class of business.

JAPAN

I. Regulations concerning the supervision of solvency

Insurance supervisory authorities stated three regulations to directly secure solvency of insurance companies.

These regulations are about:

– conservative reserving policy;
– conservative method on asset valuation; and
– the method of utilising assets.

Also, the authorities stated other regulations to indirectly secure solvency of insurance companies. These regulations are about:

– obtaining a licence for conducting insurance business;
– prohibition of carrying on other business and prohibition of carrying on both life and non-life insurance business;
– raising funds; and
– obtaining approval on dividends to policyholders in life insurance companies and non-life mutual companies.

A. *Conservative reserving policy*

To ensure sound operation of insurance business, the Japanese Authorities require insurance companies to observe conservative reserving policy. It is regulated that life insurance companies should make policy reserves with the net level premium method, and contingency reserves in preparation for a disaster by Article 88 of the Insurance Business Law, Article 31 of the Enforcement Regulations of the Insurance Business Law and a Ministry of Finance's order. On the other hand, it is stated that non-life insurance companies should set aside a catastrophe loss reserve in excess of ordinary reserves (unearned premium reserves) in Article 88 of the Insurance Business Law, Article 13-2 of the Enforcement Regulations and a Ministry of Finance's order. In addition to the above, both life and non-life insurance companies should set aside net capital gain accruing from sale of insurers' assets as stated in Article 86 of the Insurance Business Law in preparation for a future decline of asset value.

B. Conservative method on asset valuation

It is stated in a Ministry of Finance's order that insurance companies have to use lower-of-cost-or-market-principle to value listed securities. As a result, the unrealised gains are the collateral for claims paying ability of insurance companies.

C. The method of utilising assets

In order for insurance companies to diversify investment risks and secure liquidity of assets, restrictions on the method of utilising asset and limitations on utilisation of assets are stated in Article 14, 18, 19, and 20 of the Enforcement Regulations of the Insurance Business Law and a Ministry of Finance's order. The above order states a current asset ratio for non-life insurance companies to secure liquidity of assets. Based on those regulations, both life and non-life insurance companies prepare ''the statement showing the methods of utilising assets'', which describes the types of assets can be held and ceilings imposed on holding assets. This is one of the fundamental documents insurance companies have to submit in order to obtain a licence for insurance business. Any change in ''the statement showing the method of utilising assets'' is subject to approval of the Ministry of Finance.

D. Other regulations

1. Obtaining licence for conducting insurance business

Article 1 of Insurance Business Law states that insurance business in Japan cannot be conducted without a licence in order to protect the interest of policyholders.

2. Prohibition of carrying on other business and carrying on both life and non-life insurance business by a company

Article 5 of Insurance Business Law prohibits carrying on other business in principle in fear of affecting the protection of policyholders in case of failing operation of other business. Article 7 of Insurance Business Law prohibited carrying on both life and non-life insurance business in order not to hurt policyholders in case of loss. For instance, a loss incurred by carrying on non-life insurance business should not be covered by a profit accrued by carrying on life insurance business.

3. Raising funds

The methods of raising funds of insurance companies are limited to a repurchase agreement of bonds or an overdraft loan to avoid its assets to be affected by risks from raising funds.

4.   Obtaining approval on dividends to policyholders in life insurance companies and non-life mutual companies

A Ministry of Finance's order states dividends for policyholders of all life insurance companies and mutual non-life insurance companies have to be approved in advance for the sound operation of the business.

II.   Practical organisation of the supervision

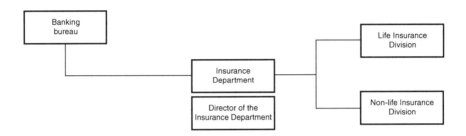

MINISTRY OF FINANCE

III.   Measures taken when an insurance company is in financially difficult condition (measures for reconstruction)

A.   *Measures taken by the competent Minister's order*

1.   Supervisory order (Article 9 of the Insurance Business Law)

The competent Minister may order an insurance company, when he considers that such order is necessary in view of the conditions of business or assets of an insurance company, to alter its method of carrying on business or to deposit its assets with a deposit office or may issue any other necessary supervisory order to it. Some of the actual cases include the deposit of assets, the obligation of prior approval for overseas remittance and prohibition of taking out from the office documents relating to the insurance transactions.

2.   Alternations in fundamental documents (Paragraph 2 and 3 of Article 10 of the Insurance Business Law)

The competent Minister may order an insurance company to make alteration in the particulars stated in the documents for licence, when he considers that such order is necessary in view of the conditions of business or assets of an insurance company or in view of change of circumstances. The competent Minister may impose the condition that such alteration shall apply for future to any existing insurance but also under Paragraph 3 of Article 10, he may impose to raise premiums for the existing insurance.

3. *Competent Minister's recommendation of amalgamation, entrusting with management or transfer of portfolio* (Article 99 of the Insurance Business Law)

When, in view of the conditions of business or assets of an insurance company, the competent Minister considers it appropriate to cause the company to be amalgamated with another company, to entrust another company with the management of its business and assets or to transfer its portfolio to another company, he may so recommend to the company. (However, there is no legal obligation for the insurance company to comply with this recommendation).

4. *Competent Minister's order of suspension of business, compulsory management or transfer of portfolio* (Article 100 of the Insurance Business Law)

When, in view of the conditions of business or assets of an insurance company, the competent Minister considers that it is difficult for the insurance company to continue its business or, in view of unsatisfactory conditions of its business, he considers that the continuation of its business is detrimental to the public interest, he may order the company to suspend its business or to transfer the management of its business and assets or its portfolio to another company.

a) When an insurance company is ordered *to suspend its business,* the company is prohibited to solicit new contracts, transact business other than insurance, or sell its assets. This is an emergency measure to prevent new insureds and others from incurring losses by such operation.

b) When an insurance company is ordered *to do compulsory management of its business and assets,* the competent Minister may appoint an insurance custodian, who takes responsibility for management on behalf of the company. An insurance custodian shall have the power, on behalf of the company placed under compulsory management, to transact its business relating to insurance contracts and other matters and to manage and dispose of its assets, and if necessary, to amalgamate and to transfer its portfolio. The competent Minister may give necessary orders relating to management to the insurance custodian or the company placed under compulsory management and dismiss the insurance custodian, when he considers it necessary.

c) When an insurance company is ordered *to transfer of portfolio,* the company shall discuss with the designated insurance company to which its contracts are transferred, or other insurance company after obtaining approval thereon from the competent Minister when no company is designated. The resolution for transfer of portfolio shall take effect after the approval thereof has been obtained from the competent Minister. In case discussions were not made, could not be made or no agreement was reached between the companies concerned in respect of transfer of portfolio, the competent Minister may make decisions which are necessary for executing the transfer of portfolio, and the transfer of portfolio shall be effective by his decision. In case of an order of compulsory management and transfer of portfolio, the competent Minister may make alteration in the bases of calculation of underwriting reserve, etc., reduction in the insured amounts, and reduction in the premiums or alteration in the terms and conditions of the contracts for the future in respect of the existing insurance contracts of the company which are placed under compulsory management or transfer of portfolio, when he considers it necessary.

B. *Measures taken by insurance companies*

An insurance company may improve the condition of assets by making an alteration in the particulars stated in the documents upon the approval from the competent Minister. (Paragraph 1 of Article 10 of the Insurance Business Law.)

A mutual company may reduce the insured amount based on its articles of incorporation, regardless of the order by the competent Minister. (Article 46 of the Insurance Business Law, a stock company is not allowed to do this.)

An insurance company may, upon the approval from the competent Minister, entrust another insurance company with management of its business and assets. (Article 92 and after of the Insurance Business Law.) This means a complete entrust of the management.

An insurance company may transfer its portfolio to another insurance company upon the approval from the competent Minister. In case of the transfer of portfolio, the company may stipulate, in the contract of transfer, for alteration in the bases of working out of underwriting reserve, etc., reduction in the insured amounts, reduction in the premiums or alteration in the terms and conditions for the future in respect of the insurance contracts to be transferred.

An insurance company may amalgamate with another insurance company upon the approval from the competent Minister. It may provide, in the contract of amalgamation, for alteration in the bases of working out of underwriting reserve, etc., or alteration in the terms and conditions for the future in respect of the insurance contracts.

GRAND DUCHY OF LUXEMBURG

I. Supervision of insurance companies' solvency margin

Financial supervision consists in verifying that insurance companies are solvent in all their activities and that they maintain technical reserves, including mathematical reserves, and corresponding assets in compliance with the regulations and practices of the Grand Duchy of Luxemburg and EC provisions.

A. *Solvency margin legislation*

Luxemburg's solvency margin legislation is in line with Economic Union directives. Each insurance company in Luxemburg engaged in direct risk insurance in either life or non-life classes must maintain an adequate solvency margin for all of its activities.

1. *Components of the solvency margin*

The solvency margin corresponds to the company's assets free of any foreseeable liabilities, less any intangible items. In particular it includes:
- the company's paid-up share capital or, for mutual associations, the actual initial fund;
- half of the portion of the share capital or the initial fund which has not been paid up once the paid-up portion reaches 25 per cent of the capital or fund;
- statutory and free reserves;
- retained earnings;
- supplementary contributions for mutual and mutual-type companies (under the conditions laid down by law);
- capital gains resulting from an undervaluation of assets or an overvaluation of liabilities upon request and with justification (under the conditions laid down by law).

2. *Special provisions for life insurance*

Special provisions for life insurance lay down that the solvency margin may also include:
- an amount representing 50 per cent of future earnings;

87

– in the case of non-zillmerisation or of zillmerisation which does not cover the loading for acquisition costs contained in the premium, the difference between the non-zillmerised or partially zillmerised mathematical reserve and a mathematical reserve zillmerised at a rate equal to the loading for acquisition costs contained in the premium.

3.   *The amount of the solvency margin*

For non-life insurance, the amount of the solvency margin is determined by reference to the annual amount of premiums or contributions or to the average burden of losses for the last three or seven financial years depending on the risks covered.

For life insurance, the minimum solvency margin must be equal to a given fraction of the mathematical reserves and a fraction of the capital at risk.

4.   *The guarantee fund*

One-third of the minimum solvency margin constitutes the guarantee fund which may not be lower than certain amounts set by law.

One-half of the guarantee fund must consist of:

a) *the company's assets* free of any foreseeable liabilities, less any intangible items. In particular it includes:
   – the company's paid-up share capital or, for mutual companies, the actual initial fund;
   – half of the portion of share capital or the initial fund which has not been paid up once the paid-up portion reaches 25 per cent of the capital or fund;
   – statutory and free reserves;
   – retained earnings.
b) *reserves of profits*, to the extent that these reserves can be used to cover future losses and that they are not earmarked for distribution to policyholders.

B.   *Technical reserves*

All insurance companies must build up adequate technical reserves.

The technical reserves comprise:

1.   *For non-life classes of business:*

– the loss reserve and the reserve for outstanding risks;
– the loss reserve corresponds to the total estimated cost that the company would have to bear to settle all claims incurred, whether reported or not, by the end of the financial year, less the sums already paid for these claims;
– the reserve for outstanding risks is calculated on the basis of the premiums written, less cancellations and refunds, with an abatement for costs which may not exceed a rate set by the Insurance Commission.

2. For life insurance:

- the mathematical reserve and the premium reserve;
- the mathematical reserve is calculated using actuarial rules and according to the bases registered for each premium rate at the time of licensing;
- the premium reserve is calculated in terms of valuation premiums.

3. Finally, for credit insurance:

- the stabilisation reserve, which is calculated using one of the two methods proposed by the Commission.

Technical reserves are calculated on a per contract basis or, if that is not possible, using flat-rate methods.

Technical reserves must at all times be covered by equivalent and matching assets. However insurance companies may hold non-matching assets to cover an amount not exceeding 20 per cent of their liabilities in a given currency. The nature of the assets and rules for determining their amounts are laid down in a regulation.

All insurance companies must keep a permanent record of each separate class of business. This consists of a register in which all assets intended to cover technical reserves are recorded. At the end of each quarter all the assets entered into this register must be equal at least to the value of the technical reserves.

All the assets covering technical reserves constitute a separate set of assets which are used specifically to guarantee the payment of the liabilities which result from direct insurance contracts.

If these separate assets are inadequate, liabilities can only be paid by reducing the share of separate assets held by policyholders, the insured or beneficiaries, who retain a secured claim on the insurance company's surplus.

C. Shareholdings in excess of specific thresholds and the identity of shareholders

Companies operating in Luxemburg are required to notify the Insurance Commission of acquisitions or sales of equity which increase or decrease their capital beyond thresholds of 20, 33 or 50 per cent. They must inform the Commission at least once a year of the identity of shareholders or partners holding shares in excess of the specific thresholds and of the amounts involved.

II. Practical organisation of financial supervision

The following forms are used in conducting financial supervision:

- The annual profit and loss account form.
- The annual solvency margin statement form.
- The periodical continuous inventory statements:

- the *annual statement* which provides a summary of the assets covering reserves and a detailed list of assets by category of investment;
- the *quarterly statement,* which lists the assets covering the technical reserves recorded in the register. This quarterly statement must show for all categories of assets the value of the assets allocated at the end and at the beginning of the quarter.

Each insurance company is required to submit an external audit carried out annually at the company's expense by an independent auditor chosen from the list authorised by the Insurance Commission. The auditors' report is sent to the Commission.

The Insurance Commission can ask companies to provide any information and documents it requires to evaluate insurance operations in general, and can also carry out inspections at the place of business.

III. Measures to be taken when difficulties arise (recovery measures)

The Commission requires a recovery plan to be drawn up if the solvency margin is below the prescribed minimum, and a short-term financing plan if the solvency margin no longer covers the guarantee fund. The recovery plan and the short-term financing plan must be submitted to the Commission for approval.

When a company does not maintain adequate technical reserves or if these reserves are not covered at all times by equivalent and matching assets, the Commission can prohibit it from freely disposing of its assets.

The Commission can impose fines on authorised insurance companies.

Furthermore, the Commission can take disciplinary action. It can:

- issue a warning or reprimand;
- prohibit a company from carrying out certain operations or impose other restrictions on its activities;
- temporarily suspend one or several of the company's managers.

MEXICO

The Mexican Constitution establishes that the Federal Government, through Congress, has the authority to regulate all issues concerning financial services, and the "Secretaría de Hacienda y Crédito Público" (SHCP: Ministry of the Treasury) is responsible for regulating the financial sector.

The supervisory authority is a decentralised federal agency of the SHCP, created in 1990: the "Comisión Nacional de Seguros y Fianzas" (CNSF).

I. Solvency regulation

A. *Minimum paid capital*

The minimum paid capital is constituted in order to guarantee the solvency of a company. It is determined in the first quarter of each year by the SHCP, taking into account the largest of:

- 1 per cent of the aggregate paid capital and capital reserves of all the companies in the previous year; and
- the last year minimum paid capital brought into the present by the inflation index.

B. *Rates*

Insurance companies are free to set the rates and conditions for their services. However, they must register each product at the CNSF with a technical note. This registration is automatic, *i.e.,* the companies can sell the product immediately. The CNSF has 30 days to provide any comment on its feasibility, and can always stop the sale of a product if it is jeopardising the solvency of the carrier.

C. *Reserves*

For life insurance, the mathematical reserve for traditional products must be constituted according to mortality tables issues by the SHCP and an interest rate less than or equal to 8 per cent.

The unearned premium reserve for health, accident and general insurance, except earthquake, is constituted by subtracting the acquisition expenses for the premiums, according to the 1/24 methodology.

The reserve for pending claims is constituted for losses and matured policies, dividends on policies and for incurred but not reported claims.

An equalisation reserve, called "reserva de previsión" (prevision reserve), must be constituted. It is accumulative and tax free-up to 50 per cent of the required solvency margin surplus. The prevision reserve can only be used by an insurance company for extraordinary losses, with the previous authorisation of the CNSF.

For earthquake, a tax deductible catastrophic risk reserve must be accumulated.

For some lines of business, in which periodic deviations in the loss ratio are likely to occur such as agriculture, cattle, and traveller's insurance, a special contingency reserve must be constituted.

D. Solvency margin

The required surplus as solvency margin, named Gross Solvency Requirement (GSR), is determined in a similar way as in the European Union.

The GSR is equal to the capital required for probable deviations in the retained losses and/or adverse fluctuations in the price of those assets in which the technical reserves are invested.

The GSR is calculated separately for life, health and accident, motor vehicle and jointly for all the other general lines.

For life insurance, the GSR is equal to 0.03 per cent of the averaged sum insured of the last 12 months.

For health and accident, motor vehicle and general insurance, the GSR is calculated using two different methodologies: one according to the premiums written in the last 12 months, and another according to the annual average losses suffered during the last three years.

For health and accident insurance, the GSR is equal to the largest of 24 per cent of the premiums for the last 12 months and 38 per cent of the annual average losses suffered during the last three years, each multiplied by the maximum between 0.84 and the company's retention ratio.

For motor vehicle insurance, the GSR is equal to the largest of 35 per cent of the premiums for the last 12 months and 48 per cent of the annual average losses suffered during the last three years, each multiplied by the maximum between 0.95 and the company's retention ratio.

For general insurance, the GSR is equal to the largest of 34 per cent of the premiums of the last twelve months and 54 per cent of the annual average losses suffered during the last three years, each multiplied by the maximum between 0.31 and the company's retention ratio.

The GSR must be less than or equal to the sum of the prevision reserve and the policyholders surplus. However, a company is only required to constitute the prevision reserve gradually over time, up to 50 per cent of the GSR.

E. Investments

There is a list of authorised securities, as well as investment limits according to the type of assets and to the issuer of the financial instrument. The regulation applies only to those investments that support the contingent liabilities of policyholders (technical reserves). A minimum percentage has to be invested in short term financial instruments, defined as those with a maturity period less than or equal to one year. Since 1993, investments are valued and disclosed to the general public at market prices.

II. Supervision

A. Supervision by the CNSF

The CNSF has a financial and actuarial area responsible for supervising the insurance companies, based on information they provide during the year.

The CNSF publishes several periodicals including the following information: financial statements and ratios, solvency margins, premiums and claims per company and line of business, and statistical information per insurance line.

Besides, the CNSF publishes twice per year a consumers information bulletin, including the number of complaints filed at the CNSF per company, with respect to their premiums and claims.

B. Supervision by external auditors

Insurance companies are required to be examined each year by independent financial examiners and actuaries.

The independent financial examiners verifies the accuracy of the financial statements and is responsible of notifying to the CNSF any anomaly or problem in the carrier.

Currently, the independent actuary reports to the CNSF the adequacy of the mathematical reserve for life insurance, and from December of 1994, companies will also have to report the sufficiency of all technical reserves.

III. Measures to be taken with problem companies

Whenever the guarantee capital (policyholders surplus) of an insurance company falls below the minimum amount required, the company must submit a plan for restoring its financial position. This plan, if authorised by the CNSF, must be accomplished within 6 months at the most.

If the company does not comply within that time, the CNFS's Board of Governors may take any of the following measures:

- grant it a fixed period of time, which cannot be extended, to be adequately capitalised;
- grant it a term to become a mutual society;
- dissolved it and transfer its business to another firm; or
- take over its administration.

NETHERLANDS

I. Introduction

Generally speaking supervision of insurance companies aims at the protection of the interests of – present and future – policyholders and insurance claimants. The general goal is to minimise the risk that the insurance company cannot meet its commitments to its insured. One of the instruments to realise this goal is solvency control.

This note provides in a nutshell an overview of the way solvency control of insurance companies is exercised in the Netherlands. Section II contains some background information on the history and nature of the Dutch system of supervision. In Section III the solvency regulations in the Netherlands are presented. Section IV deals with the way in which the Dutch Supervisory Authority, the Verzekeringskamer (Insurance Board) organises solvency control. Finally, Section V describes the measures that can be taken when solvency difficulties arise.

II. The Dutch system of insurance supervision

The legal supervision of insurance companies in the Netherlands originates from 1922, when the Life Insurance Companies Act passed Parliament. In pursuance of this Act the Insurance Board started its work in 1923. Some 40 years later, in 1964, by virtue of a separate Act, non-life insurers were also placed under supervision of the Insurance Board. In implementing the First Life Insurance Directive (Directive 79/267/EC) and the First Non-life Insurance Directive (73/239/EC) in 1987 one integrated legal system of supervision of life and non-life insurance companies was created: the Wet toezicht verzekeringsbedrijf (the Insurance Business Supervision Act, IBSA). By virtue of separate Acts the Insurance Board also supervises private pension funds in the Netherlands.

From the very beginning the Dutch supervisory system can be characterised as normative. This means that there are no restrictions as to the management of an insurance company (policy conditions, tariffs, investments, etc.), provided that the company meets certain legal standards. The core of this system is solvency control. It is completed by comprehensive annual accounts to be submitted to the Insurance Board. With the exception of certain confidential information, which might – for instance – disturb competition among insurance companies, these accounts must be disclosed. It is the conviction of the

Dutch Government and also of the Insurance Board that this normative system of supervision serves the interests of the policyholders and claimants best, while at the same time restricting competition among insurance companies as little as possible. This system is believed to pursue a balance between regulation and freedom to manage an insurance company, which aims at optimising the safeguard for policyholders and claimants. A maximum safeguard, *i.e.,* the exclusion of winding-up of an insurance company, cannot be guaranteed, however. It should be noted that the Third Non-life Insurance Directive (Directive 92/49/EC) and the Third Life Insurance Directive (Directive 92/96/EC) are by and large based on these principles. Within the normative system of control the Insurance Board has several administrative powers at its disposal to influence the management of the insurance company in the interest of policyholders and claimants. The IBSA regulates that the board of managing directors of an insurance company must consist of at least two persons. Members of the board of managing directors should have adequate expertise. Their fitness and properness are assessed by the Insurance Board. Moreover, public limited companies must have a board of supervisory directors consisting of at least three persons. Insurance companies are obliged to supply the Insurance Board with any information it needs for its supervisory tasks. This obligation also applies to affiliated companies, being part of a group to which the insurance company belongs. Participations by an insurance company in a bank of more than 5 per cent are not allowed unless a certificate of no objection has been granted by the Ministry of Finance. The same applies to a participation by a bank in an insurance company (or a holding company of a group to which an insurance company belongs) of more than 10 per cent.

Recently a tripartite agreement has been concluded by the Ministry of Finance, the Dutch Central Bank and the Insurance Board, regarding the joint supervision of Financial Conglomerates. The insurance Board has the power to give an administrative directive regarding any aspect of the management of the insurance company. The company in question has to comply with this directive. If the Insurance Board is of the opinion that the insurance company does not comply with the administrative directive it may, by way of sanction, disclose the directive in the Official Gazette. The Insurance Board may also appoint one or more persons whose consent (members of) the board of managing directors need when effecting their powers (so called hidden trustees(s)).

To conclude this section some factual information on the Dutch insurance environment is presented.

By the end of 1992, 97 authorised life insurance companies, of which 87 Dutch assurance companies and 10 branches of foreign assurance companies were active in the Dutch market. Their gross premium income amounted to Gld 24.1 billion (1991); Gld 22.6 billion was accounted for by the Dutch assurers and Gld 1.5 billion by the foreign assurers. The respective balance sheet totals amounted to (billions of Gld) 221.8 and 9.5, in total 231.3. The solvency margin of the Dutch life assurers was about 9 per cent of the net technical provisions, this being about 190 per cent of the required margin.

By the end of 1992 391 authorised non-life insurance companies, of which 251 Dutch insurance companies and 140 branches of foreign insurance companies were active on the Dutch market. Their gross premium income (1991) amounted to (billions of Gld) 20.2, of which 18.8 for the account of the Dutch insurers and 1.4 of the branches of foreign insurers. The respective balance sheet totals amounted to 35.3 and 3.1, in total 38.4. The solvency margin of the Dutch non-life insurers was about 52 per cent of the gross premiums, this being about 350 per cent of the required margin.

In 1992 the Insurance Board employed 110 persons, 21 of which were employed at the Insurance Department. This Department is primarily responsible for the supervision of insurance companies.

III. Solvency regulations

As indicated before solvency control lies at the heart of the Dutch system of supervision of insurance companies. The solvency regulations of the Netherlands are in agreement with the respective First EC Directives: Articles 16 and 17 of the Directive 73/239/EC and Articles 18-20 of the Directive 79/267/EC. Although these regulations constitute the basis of the Dutch solvency control, the story does not end here. Solvency is by nature connected with the calculation and valuation of assets and liabilities of the insurance company. According to the mentioned EC Directives (Article 15 of the Directive 73/239/EC and Article 17 of the Directive 79/267/EC) the IBSA regulates that the insurance company must have adequate technical provisions, which have to be fully covered by assets. As to the technical provisions, more detailed rules are laid down in a Royal Decree, which delegates some discretionary powers to the Insurance Board.

The technical provisions for life insurance have to be calculated on the basis of prudent actuarial assumptions and rates of interest. In general a rate of interest of more than 4 per cent is not accepted by the Insurance Board. However, for some specific products a rate of interest based on the returns on related investments is allowed. A Zillmer percentage of more than 2 per cent is generally not accepted. In calculating provisions for immediate annuities only recently based mortality tables are acceptable.

As set out in Section II there is no *a priori* supervision of tariffs. However, the Insurance Board may assess that the actuarial assumptions or interest rates, which were used in calculating those tariffs, fall short of prudent standards, which the Board thinks necessary when calculating the technical provisions. In that case the Insurance Board may urge the insurance company to create supplementary provisions, to be debited to the profit and loss account. For instance in this field a general administrative directive of the Insurance Board is in force, which states that for with-profit policies with guaranteed profit shares a provision for the full amount of the profit share shall be built up within 15 years.

In pursuance of the IBSA the Insurance Board may object against the nature and the valuation of the assets covering the technical provisions, with which objections the insurance company must comply. It should be well understood that within the framework of the system of supervision, as set out in Section II, there are no specific investment rules. Investment portfolios should comply with prudent standards of diversification, profitability, liquidity and solidity. In principle the valuation of assets should be in accordance with general accepted standards within the branch of industry. The IBSA regulates that reinsurance debtors may be accepted as assets covering the technical provisions in so far as there are no counter claims.

Regarding the technical provisions of non-life insurers and the assets covering these provision – as far as relevant – the same applied as is stated before relating to life insurance companies. According to Directive 73/239/EC for the credit insurance class an equalisation provision is applicable. This provision must be calculated on the basis of the second method of Annex D of the directive. The Insurance Board has ruled that if an insurer sells health insurance policies with a tariff based on actuarial assumptions, the insurer must use specified accounting schemes when creating technical provisions for these policies.

As is well known the Third Life Insurance Directive (Directive 92/96/EC, Articles 18-24) and the Third Non-life Insurance Directive (Directive 92/49/EC, Articles 17-23) contain more detailed regulations as to the calculation and valuation of the technical provisions and of the assets covering these provisions. These regulations will be implemented in to the Dutch insurance legislation by 1 June 1994.

IV. The organisation of solvency control

The Insurance Department of the Insurance Board is primarily responsible for the supervision of insurance companies. The Insurance Department has six Account Managers, each of whom is primarily responsible for the supervision of a number of insurance companies. The Account Manager is generally a Registered Auditor or an Actuary. Employees of the Department are trained in the field of either the auditing or the actuarial discipline. Legal expertise is supplied by the Advisory and Research Department.

Apart from the formal and legal procedures in authorising an insurance company, the supervision of insurance companies is effected in two ways. Firstly, every year a thorough analysis is made of the annual accounts which the insurance company must submit to the Insurance Board. Secondly, every 3-5 years on-the-spot investigations are carried out.

The annual accounts are submitted in the form of prescribed forms, relating to the balance sheet and the profit and loss account, the investments, the technical provisions and the technical and financial results. For life insurance companies and for some classes of non-life insurance a report on an Actuary is required. The complete set of forms, presenting the annual accounts, are certified by an External Auditor.

The fact that the reports of the Actuary and the External Auditor both constitute an integral part of the annual accounts, influences the level of analysis of the accounts. Detailed checks of a variety of elements of the annual accounts is not executed by the Insurance Department. The overall analysis aims at gaining an adequate opinion on the solvency of the insurance company. Investigations are made into the technical provisions, the assumptions on which these are calculated and the run-off of provisions, the investments, and the technical and financial results. Moreover, these results are analysed over the past five financial years. If assessed necessary specific aspects of the annual accounts are subjected to more detailed analyses. Minor points resulting from the analysis of the annual accounts are communicated in writing to the insurance company. Result which might influence the solvency of the insurance company are discussed with the board of managing directors of the company.

Results of the analysis of the annual accounts may have an impact on the programme for the on-the-spot investigation of the insurance company, which are carried out every 3-5years. On the occasion of such an investigation different aspects of the annual accounts and in a broader sense of the management of the insurance company are subjected to more thorough analyses. These may include the insurance policy, the technical provisions (assumptions, run-off), technical and financial results, and so on. Also the – short and long term – policy of the management of the insurance company is analysed. The results of these investigations are discussed with the board of managing directors of the insurance company in question.

In concluding this section some recent developments regarding the supervision of insurance companies are being passed in review. First of all, the Insurance Department intends to intensify its supervision of the insurance companies. Each year the Account Managers will visit every insurance company by way of a mini on-the-spot investigation (1-3 days visit). Subjects for discussion may be the results of the analysis of the annual accounts of the insurance company, the policy of the insurance company and recent developments relating to the company. Secondly, some years ago the Insurance Board started a project aimed at ''computerising'' the annual accounts of the insurance companies. By now insurance companies have the opportunity to submit their annual accounts on disk, which is put into a database of the Insurance Board. On this basis the analysis of the annual accounts can be intensified. Thirdly, recently some experience has been gained with Early Warning Systems. This is a computerised system of checks and balances based on a ratio-analysis of the annual accounts. The Research and Advisory Department is doing more research in this field. This department recently also started a research project on Embedded Values of insurance companies. Among other things, it is investigated if elements of the EV-analysis can be used as a tool in the assessment of the future solvency of insurance companies.

V. Measures when difficulties arise

Apart from the occurrence of catastrophes, difficulties with which an insurance company might be confronted are usually predictable. It is the aim of solvency control, and in a broader sense of supervision of insurance companies, to minimise the risk that such predictable difficulties, that might endanger the survival of the insurance company, would occur. With this objective in mind, in the day-to-day supervision of insurance companies all kinds of signals may come up, which might indicate that difficulties could occur. Such signals may be the result of the analysis of the annual accounts, of on-the-spot investigations or of any other information made available to the Insurance Board.

In assessing these signals the Insurance Board may make enquiries of the insurance company. If necessary the subject is discussed with the board of managing directors of the insurance company. These enquiries or discussions may lead to the conclusion that specific measures are called for. If the company is not convinced of the necessity to take these measures, the Insurance Board may urge it to take them. The ultimate power of the

Insurance Board, as set out in Section II, is to give an administrative directive with which the insurance company must comply. Such a directive may regard any aspect of the management of the insurance company, such as for instance: the calculation and valuation of technical provision and the partition and valuation of assets.

More serious problems arise when the solvency of the insurance company falls short of the required margin or the required minimum of the guarantee fund according to the relevant EC Directives. The respective regulations (Article 20 of the Directive 73/239/EC and Article 24 of the Directive 79/267/EC) are incorporated in the IBSA.

According to these rules the insurance company has to submit a plan for the restoration of a sound financial position respectively a short term finance scheme, which are to be approved by the Insurance Board. The latter may also restrict or prohibit the free disposal of the assets of the insurance company. If the measures mentioned above do not suffice, the Insurance Board may withdraw the authorisation of the insurance company. Consequently, the insurance company must liquidate its business, still being supervised by the Insurance Board. If the Insurance Board thinks it necessary, it may, in the interest of all the creditors of the insurance company, petition the Court within whose jurisdiction the insurance company has its registered office, to declare the Emergency Rules of the IBSA applicable. According to these Rules the Insurance Board is authorised by the Court to liquidate all or part of the insurance portfolio, or to transfer the insurance portfolio of the insurance company. Under these Rules the Insurance Board also has the power to liquidate the insurance company.

If the Insurance Board does not succeed in liquidating or transferring the insurance portfolio of the insurance company, it may petition the Court to declare the insurance company bankrupt. From then on the Bankruptcy Act will be applicable. A Trustee appointed by the Court will wind up the business of the insurance company, according to the regulations of the Bankruptcy Act.

NEW ZEALAND

Introduction

There are two separate private insurance supervision regimes in operation in New Zealand – one in respect of fire and general insurance, and the other in respect of life insurance. Both regimes have been in place since last century and both are presently under review, with the aim of updating them to cope with the issues raised in the modern commercial environment. The enactment of the Accident Compensation Act 1972, which provides for compensation by the State for personal injury by accident, rendered compulsory insurance against worker injury or death by employers and third party insurance against injury or death non-existent in New Zealand.

I. Fire and general insurance

The supervisory regime for fire and general insurers is located in both the Insurance Companies Deposits Act 1953 and the Companies Act 1955.

A. *Insurance Companies Deposits Act 1953*

This Act provides:

a) All persons commencing insurance business after 28 August 1976 (with the exception of life insurance and business insurance) are obliged to pay a NZ$5 000 deposit to the Public Trustee.

b) Mutual assurance associations carrying out employer's liability insurance must deposit securities of not less than NZ$2 000, plus further approved securities of not less than NZ$2 000 per every NZ$5 000 or premium income, up to a maximum of NZ$45 000.

c) Companies carrying on fidelity guarantee insurance or personal indemnity insurance, and no other class of insurance business, may be exempted from the deposit requirements.

d) Persons required to make a deposit must prepare, in the form prescribed, the following accounts at the expiration of each financial year:
   - underwriting account;
   - investment account;

- profit and loss account;
- appropriation account;
- balance sheet.

Each account is to be audited and filed with the Department of Justice.

B. Companies Act 1955

This Act provides:

a) Companies carrying on in a New Zealand insurance business, other than life insurance, must maintain paid up capital intact of not less than NZ$100 000.

b) Companies insuring the property of their own members and no other person must maintain issued capital of NZ$100 000, and paid up capital intact of NZ$50 000.

c) Companies carrying on in New Zealand insurance business must, once in every year that they carry on such business, file a balance sheet with the Registrer of Companies.

d) Overseas companies carrying on insurance business in New Zealand must have a paid up capital intact of at least NZ$100 000 unless they keep a sum of not less than NZ$100 000 deposited with the Public Trustee (including any deposit paid under the Insurance Companies Deposits Act 1953).

e) The Minister of Justice has the power to authorise an inspection of insurance companies of doubtful solvency, and petition for the winding-up of an insurance company on the ground that it is insolvent.

C. Solvency monitoring by the insurance industry

As an informal measure, the Insurance Council of New Zealand Inc. monitors the solvency of its own members. Achievement of a satisfactory solvency ratio is a prerequisite for continued membership of the Insurance Council. It should be noted however that not all insurance companies in New Zealand are members of the Council.

D. Review of fire and general insurance

As well as the recognition that the supervisory regime for fire and general insurance is in need of updating, two significant developments have added to the impetus for change. The first is the reduction of public insurance of earthquake and disaster risk, by the gradual transfer of all risk for non-residential property to the private sector. Legislation effecting this reform is expected to be passed at any time. The second is the comprehensive reform of companies legislation in New Zealand. It is expected that the new legislation will come into force on 1 July 1994, and the draft legislation has discarded all provisions relating to insurance companies, which will form part of a separate piece of stand-along legislation. The precise contents of such stand-along legislation are not yet known; discussion papers have raised concepts such as the imposition of a requirement to obtain and maintain a satisfactory rating from a private sector rating agency, the abolition of statutory deposits and more detailed and meaningful reporting requirements.

II. Life insurance

The relevant provisions in relation to life insurance are found in the Life Insurance Act 1908 and the Securities Act 1978.

A. Life Insurance Act 1908

The Life Insurance Act:

a) Requires life insurers to deposit approved securities of not less than NZ$500 000 with Public Trustee.

b) Requires life insurers to maintain solely for the security of life policy and annuity holders, a separate life insurance fund, consisting of all receipt in respect of the life insurance and annuity contracts of the company. This requirement applies where a life insurer transacts other insurance besides life insurance.

c) Requires life insurers, at the expiration of each financial year, to deposit the following financial statements with the Secretary of Justice:
- revenue account;
- balance sheet;
- profit and loss account;
- statement of loss and annuity business.

In addition, the companies must file certain statements made by an actuary:
- valuation of the liabilities under life policies and annuities;
- consolidated revenue account;
- summary and valuation of policies;
- valuation balance sheet.

B. The Securities Act 1978

This Act provides, among other things, specific rules governing the offer and allotment of securities. The definition of securities in the Act is very wide, and covers most forms of investment. Life insurance bonds and like investment products are considered to be securities. The Act contains a specific provision permitting life insurers to apply for an exemption from the restrictions imposed by the Act. It also permits the Securities Commission (which administers the Act) to impose standards and reporting requirements on the life insurer as a condition of granting the exemption.

C. Review

A review of the provisions of the Life Insurance Act 1908 is presently underlay. Proposals under discussion include updating the reporting requirements to ensure that financial statements provide more meaningful information, and introduction of an appointed actuary regime similar to that presently in operation in Australia. Any legislative reform is unlikely to be enacted for at least twelve months.

D. *Other relevant legislation*

The following statutes also impact upon the supervision of private insurers:

Statute	Effect
Mutual Insurance Act 1955	Provides for incorporation and operation of mutual insurance associations
Marine Insurance Act 1908	Regulates conduct of marine insurance
Insurance Law Reform Acts 1977 and 1985	Reforms certain law governing contracts of insurance

NORWAY

I. Regulation No. 875 of 22 October 1990; Regulation on a minimum standard of capital adequacy for financial institutions

A. *Scope – Section 1*

This regulation applies to commercial banks, savings banks, other credit institutions and insurance companies, and other companies or institutions encompassed by Act No. 39 of 10 June 1988 relating to Insurance Companies and by Act No. 40 of 10 June 1988 concerning Financing Activities and Financial Institutions (The Financial Services Act).

The regulation stipulates a minimum capital ratio for institutions mentioned in the first paragraph, as well as how the basis of measurement of capital is to be calculated.

B. *Required capital ratio – Section 2*

Institutions shall at all times maintain a capital ratio of at least 8 per cent of the basis of measurement as stipulated in Section 4.

C. *Special rules for life insurance companies – Section 3*

Repealed as of 17 January 1992.

D. *The basis and method of measurement – Section 4*

The basis of measurement comprises both on-balance-sheet items and off-balance-sheet items. The various items are risk-weighted according to the credit risk they are assumed to represent. The book value of the on-balance-sheet items and the converted value of the off-balance-sheet items, of Section 6, shall be multiplied by the respective risk weight and the total arrived at constitutes the basis of measurement.

The composition of capital is subject to the provisions set out in regulation No. 435 of 1 June 1990 on the measurement of the capital of financial institutions.

E. *Risk weights assigned to asset items – Section 5*

The various asset items shall carry the following risk weights:

1. *Zero per cent*

 - cash holdings and assets of a similar nature;
 - claims on and claims guaranteed by OECD central governments and central banks;
 - claims collateralised by securities issued or guaranteed by OECD central governments or central banks;
 - claims on central governments and central banks outside the OECD that are denominated in the debtor's currency and funded in the same currency;
 - claims guaranteed by central governments and central banks outside the OECD that are denominated and funded in the guarantor's and the debtor's common currency;
 - claims collateralised by the financial institution's own borrowing;
 - claims on and claims guaranteed by Norwegian State-owned enterprises (not limited by shares).

2. *Twenty per cent*

 - claims on and claims guaranteed by multilateral developments banks;
 - claims collateralised by securities issued or guaranteed by multilateral development banks;
 - claims on and claims guaranteed by domestic financial institutions and foreign credit institutions incorporated in the OECD that are not included in these institutions' capital base;
 - claims on and claims guaranteed by banks incorporated in countries outside the OECD with an original maturity of up to one year that are not included in these institutions' capital base;
 - claims on and claims guaranteed by Norwegian municipalities;
 - claims on and claims guaranteed by non-domestic OECD public sector entities other than central governments and central banks.

3. *Fifty per cent*

 - loans secured by mortgage on residential property that is or will be occupied by the borrower or that is rented, up to 80 per cent of prudent valuation;
 - interim assets (earned income not yet due, and prepaid costs). Items that are distributed on debtor sector are given a risk weight according to the category of the counterparty.

4. *One hundred per cent*

 - all other items in the balance sheet, except items deducted from the financial institution's capital, *cf.* regulation No. 435 of 1 June 1990 on the measurement of the capital of financial institutions.

F. Units held in investment funds (shares, bonds, etc.) – Section 5A

Upon application of the rules of Section 4, second paragraph, *cf.* regulation No. 435 of 1 June 1990 on the measurement of the capital of financial institutions, and the rules of Section 5, any units held in a collective investment fund shall be regarded as direct ownership of an identical share of the assets managed by the fund:

a) if the fund's assets are confined to holdings which under Section 5 of regulation No. 875 of 22 October 1990 concerning a minimum standard of capital adequacy for financial institutions carry a risk weight of 0 per cent;

b) if the fund's assets are confined to holdings which under Section 5 of regulation No. 875 of 22 October 1990 on minimum standard of capital adequacy for financial institutions carry a risk weight of 20 per cent;

c) if the fund's assets are confined to holdings which under Section 5 of regulation No. 875 of 22 October 1990 on a minimum standard of capital adequacy for financial institutions carry a risk weight of 50 per cent;

d) to the extent that the fund's resources are invested in capital in financial institutions.

If more than 50 per cent of the fund's resources consist of holdings coming under first paragraph, litera *a); first paragraph, litera *b); or first paragraph, litera *c); the Banking, Insurance and Securities Commission may determine that the provision of the first paragraph shall apply correspondingly.

G. Off-balance-sheet-engagements – Section 6

Off-balance-sheet engagements shall be converted to credit risk equivalents by multiplying the nominal amounts by a conversion factor. The resulting amounts, *i.e.* the assumed credit risk arrived at – are then weighted directly into the calculation base using the risk weights set out in Section 5.

The following conversion factors apply:

- Direct credit substitutes (*e.g.* loan guarantees, general guarantees of indebtedness and acceptances) shall carry a 100 per cent credit risk conversion factor.
- Asset sales with a repurchase agreement and asset sales with recourse where the credit risk remains with the financial institution, and endorsed loan documents (*e.g.* rediscounted bills of exchange and instalment contracts) that do not carry the binding signature of another financial institution, shall carry a 100 per cent conversion factor. The measured credit risk is to be weighted using the risk weights – set out in Section 5 – applicable to the category of the counterparty.
- Forward asset purchases, forward forward deposits and the unpaid part of partly-paid shares and securities shall carry a conversion factor of 100 per cent. The measured credit risk in respect of forward asset purchases is to be weighted using the risk weights – set out in Section 5 – applicable to the category of the counterparty.
- Transaction-related contingent items (*e.g.* contract guarantees, payment guarantees and guarantees for tax payments) shall carry a 50 per cent conversion factor.

- Note issuance facilities and revolving underwriting facilities with an original maturity of more than one year shall have a 50 per cent conversion factor.
- Documentary credit and other trade-related contingent items shall carry a 20 per cent conversion factor.
- Other commitments with an original maturity of more than one year (e.g. formal standby facilities and credit lines with an original maturity of more than one year) shall carry a 50 per cent conversion factor. Commitments with an original maturity of less than one year, or which can be unconditionally cancelled at any time, are not to be included.

Interest and foreign exchange related instruments shall be converted to the credit equivalent amount by calculating the replacement cost in the market and adding the potential future exposure over the residual lifetime of the contract (replacement cost method). Institutions with limited trade in such instruments may with the consent of the Banking, Insurance and Securities Commission calculate the credit equivalent amount by multiplying the nominal amounts by a conversion factor depending on the original maturity (original exposure method).

H. Consolidation – Section 7

If an institution that is subject to this regulation has a holding in another financial institution representing 20 per cent or more of the equity or voting rights, the capital adequacy rules of this regulation shall also be applied on a consolidated basis, *cf.* Section 2-16 of Act No. 40 of 10 June 1988 on Financing Activities and Financial Institutions (the Financial Services Act) with appurtenant regulations. The Banking, Insurance and Securities Commission may also order consolidation in respect of holdings in companies which are not financial institutions and in respect of holdings of 10 per cent or more.

I. Supplementary rules – Section 8

The Banking, Insurance and Securities Commission may lay down further rules concerning the implementation and application of this regulation.

J. Entry into force – Section 9

This regulation enters into force on 31 March 1991. Regulation No. 435 of 1 June 1990 on the measurement of the capital of financial institutions enters into force on the same date, *cf.* Section 10.

The institutions shall calculate their capital ratio as at 31 March 1991 in accordance with the present regulation.

K. Transitional regulations – Section 10

The following transitional regulations apply:

1. *Commercial banks, savings banks and mortgage companies*

Commercial banks and mortgage companies which do not satisfy the capital adequacy requirements set out in this regulation by 31 March 1991 must satisfy the requirements of Sections 2 and 7 by 31 December 1992. Savings banks must meet the requirements of Sections 2 and 7 by 31 December 1992.

By 31 December 1991, commercial banks, savings banks and mortgage companies must raise their capital ratio by a minimum of 30 per cent of the difference between the standard of 8 per cent set out in Sections 2 and 7 and the ratio attained as at 31 March 1991.

2. *Finance companies*

Finance companies must meet the requirements under Section 2 and 7 by 31 December 1991. The capital adequacy requirement of 10 per cent as calculated under the previous rules will apply up to 31 December 1991 whereby general provisions, goodwill etc. and reserves in the leasing portfolio are not included in the capital base.

3. *Insurance companies and their parent companies*

Insurance companies and their parent companies must satisfy the requirements of Sections 2 and 7 by 31 December 1997. Insurance companies and their parent companies shall have achieved a minimum capital ratio, as calculated in accordance with the rules of this regulation, of 3.5 per cent by 31 December 1991, 4.25 per cent by 31 December 1992, 5.0 per cent by 31 December 1993, 5.75 per cent by 31 per cent December 1994, 6.75 per cent by 31 December 1995, and 7.5 per cent by 31 December 1996.

In the period between the date of the entry into force of this regulation and 31 December 1991, insurance companies and their parent companies must satisfy the capital adequacy requirements set out in Subsection 4 or Royal decree No. 835 III of 25 August 1989. Up to 31 December 1991 the definition of capital applying when Royal decree of 25 August 1989 was issued shall be applied.

The two preceding paragraphs do not apply to banks which are parent companies of credit insurance companies.

Section 6, final paragraph, of regulation No. 930 of 8 September 1989 is repealed.

II. Regulation No. 214 of 25 March 1991; Regulation on the application of capital adequacy rules on a consolidated basis

A. *Scope – Section 1*

This regulation applies to commercial banks, savings banks, other credit institutions, insurance companies and other companies or institutions which are regarded as financial institutions pursuant to Act No. 40 of 10 June 1988 on Financing Activities and Financial Institutions (the Financial Services Act).

B. The minimum capital adequacy requirement on a consolidated basis – Section 2

A financial institution shall upon application of the provisions under regulations No. 875 of 22 October 1990 concerning a minimum standard of capital adequacy for financial institutions, consolidate its holdings in accordance with these provisions and satisfy the minimum capital adequacy requirements on a consolidated basis. Upon consolidation the capital adequacy requirement applying to the parent company, including the parent company of any sub-group, shall be applied unless otherwise stipulated in the terms of the licence. The rules of this section do not apply to loan intermediation enterprises.

C. Obligation to consolidate – Section 3

A financial institution shall consolidate its holdings in accordance with these regulations when such holdings either directly or indirectly represent 20 per cent or more of the share capital or votes in:

- another Norwegian or foreign financial institution;
- a Norwegian or foreign securities house, commercial building or property company, investment trust company or any other company with substantial financial assets.

The obligation to consolidate also applies to financial institutions which are parent companies of sub-groups, as well as to collaborative mutual insurance companies and other corresponding group affiliates which are not part of an ownership hierarchy.

The Banking, Insurance and Securities Commission will, in case of doubt, decide whether the obligation to consolidate shall apply as stipulated in this section.

Upon special application the Banking, Insurance and Securities Commission may order consolidation of holdings of 10 per cent or more when such holdings are considered to constitute an extension of a financial institution's own activity.

The Banking, Insurance and Securities Commission may also completely or partially exempt a financial institution from the obligation to consolidate pursuant to this section, provided that the minimum capital adequacy requirement on a consolidated basis does not deviate significantly from the minimum capital adequacy requirement applying to the financial institution itself.

D. Consolidation principles – Section 4

Consolidation of group accounts shall be based on the principle of pro rata consolidation. Consolidation shall also include off-balance-sheet engagements. Shares in companies or institutions which are encompassed by the obligation to consolidate shall be eliminated according to the same principle as applied in the acquisition method, so that:

- the acquisition cost of the shares is eliminated against the corresponding equity capital in the institution or company at the time of acquisition;

– differences between market and book values are analysed and distributed on holdings and engagements in accordance with the principle of prudence. Goodwill and corresponding items are removed from the balance sheet and are thus not included in the total capital.

Internal assets and liabilities, internal off-balance-sheet items and intragroup income and costs among the institutions or companies subject to the obligation to consolidate shall be eliminated.

If a holding in a group company is secured by a guarantee from another group company, the guaranteed holding shall only be included once when calculating capital adequacy on a consolidated basis. Correspondingly, guarantee liability that is counter-guaranteed by another group company to which the obligation to consolidate applies shall only be measured once.

For the consolidation of holdings in foreign institutions or companies, the middle rate on the Oslo Stock Exchange on the last day of the accounting period shall be used to convert foreign currency to kroner.

E. *Entry into force – Section 5*

This regulation enters into force on 31 March 1991.

F. *Transitional provisions – Section 6*

The following transitional provisions apply:

1. *Financial Institutions*

In the period to 31 December 1991, financial institutions will be subject to a 10 per cent minimum capital ratio calculated in accordance to the rules formally enforced and on a consolidated basis.

2. *Insurance and their subsidiaries*

In the period to 31 December 1991, insurance companies and their subordinates will be subject to the minimum capital ratio set out in Subsection 4 of Royal Decree No. 825 III of 25 August 1989 on a consolidated basis.

PORTUGAL

I. General regulatory requirements

Supervision of insurance enterprises in Portugal, as in the other European countries, responds primarily to the need to protect policyholders and those entitled under them, with due regard to the specific nature of the insurance contract.

Since the reprivatisation and expansion of the insurance sector, the old system of supervising prices and products has been abandoned in favour of more stringent solvency controls.

The following are considered to be key determinants of financial solvency:

At start-up:

– adequate initial capital and a minimum guarantee fund.

In expanding business activity:

– adequate technical reserves to meet liabilities in the form of an appropriate and diversified mix of assets;
– a minimum solvency margin corresponding to uncommitted assets.

II. Specific regulatory requirements

A. *Main technical requirements*

The technical reserves are calculated gross, *i.e.* before deduction of outwards reinsurance.

The unearned premiums reserve is calculated pro rata; for some contracts it may be calculated in terms of a fixed percentage: 33.33 per cent.

The reserve for claims outstanding is calculated on a case-by-case basis and may, for particular types of risks, be calculated according to the average cost method.

The mathematical reserve is mandatorily based on mortality tables and a maximum technical zilmerisation tax may be levied.

The technical reserves are made up of assets which are subject to specific rules as to their location, scatter, diversification and evaluation criteria.

B. Capital requirements (solvency)

The minimum capital required on taking up business is Esc 1 500 million; composite (life and non-life) undertakings cannot be established.

In the case of insurance companies engaged only in suretyship insurance, insurance against recourse by third parties and legal defence, the minimum initial capital is reduced to Esc 500 million. The minimum capital requirement for mutual associations is Esc 750 million.

An insurance company must have a solvency margin proportional to turnover and commensurate with its liabilities, as well as a guarantee fund equivalent to one-third of its solvency margin.

The solvency margin and the guarantee fund – for which floor values are set – are those specified in the EC Directives in force. There are no restrictions on the investment of insurance companies' uncommitted assets.

Tariffs in non-life insurance are not controlled, but nonetheless constitute the bulk of those subject to the prior deposit requirement.

In life insurance tariffs must be submitted for prior approval. The technical bases for the calculation of mathematical reserves must be taken into account in determining premiums. (Tariffs are to be fully liberalised as from 1 July 1994.)

III. Organisation of supervision

A. Product supervision

There is systematic *ex ante* supervision of policies in the following classes: life insurance, accident insurance, credit insurance, assistance insurance, legal aid insurance and all compulsory insurance.

Other insurance policies are supervised on an *ex post* and *ad hoc* basis.

B. Financial supervision

Supervision is based on inspection of yearly financial guarantee documents and insurance companies' accounts.

Periodic audits are also undertaken, on the basis of statistical data.

Additional on-the-spot audits may be made.

Early warning signals are ensured by analysing samples of statistics deriving from checks on the adequacy of certain technical reserves and examining response ratios.

IV. Measures in case of financial insolvency

In the event that technical reserves are wrongly or inadequately calculated, insurance companies must take the necessary remedial action as stipulated by the supervisory authority.

Should the solvency margin be insufficient, an insurer must implement an approved recovery plan.

If uncommitted assets amount to less than the minimum guarantee fund, or if reserves are too low, an insurer must implement a short-term financing plan.

Failure to:

– comply with the instructions regarding the regularisation of the technical reserves,
– implement a recovery plan, or
– institute a financing plan,

triggers an administrative process which may culminate in the levying of a fine, and/or temporary suspension or withdrawal of the company's licence to do business in some or all classes of insurance.

Companies have the right to appeal to the competent Minister or to the courts, against any penalties or administrative measures that may be imposed.

If a company runs into serious financial difficulties, the Government may dismiss the board of directors and appoint a board of management.

The Government may decide to freeze the assets of any insurance company whose funds prove insufficient to meet its liabilities. In this case, the supervisory authority may refuse to license business in other classes or types of insurance activity.

If a company's difficulties are so serious that recovery is out of the question, steps are taken to wind it up.

Wind-up is decided by the judicial or administrative authorities.

In winding-up a company's assets, priority is given to meeting current liabilities towards policyholders and those entitled under them.

V. Possible changes in the system of supervision

When the third-generation EC Directives are embodied in Portuguese Law with effect from 1 July 1994, the main consequences will be:

– recognition of the principle of supervision by the country of origin and of a single authorisation enabling companies to do business throughout the European Community;
– more flexible criteria for evaluating the assets that may constitute the solvency margin;
– more flexible rules regarding the composition and distribution of assets qualifying as technical reserves;
– the end of any systematic *ex ante* supervision of policies and tariffs, including the abolishment of the prior deposit;
– closer supervision of financial conglomerates;
– tighter quality controls, particularly as regards enterprises' senior management.

SPAIN

I.   Regulations concerning the supervision of solvency

The law regarding the supervision of solvency margins is in conformity with the first EC Directives. The relevant provisions are to be found in Sections 25 and 26 of Law 33 of 2 August 1984 on Regulations for Private Insurance and in Articles 76 to 81 of Regulation 1348 of 1 August 1985.

With regard to technical provisions, the legislation (Article 24 of the Law on Regulations for Private Insurance and Articles 55 to 75 of Regulation 1348/1985) specifies the technical provisions that insurance companies are required to calculate and include in their balance sheets (mathematical provision, outstanding risk provision, claims provision, equalisation provision and unpaid premium provision), lays down the method for calculating the various technical provisions and rules which kinds of assets are allowed as technical provisions.

II.   The practical organisation of supervision

The supervision of solvency is conducted by the supervisory authorities which are a part of the Directorate-General for Insurance of the Ministry of the Economy and Finance.

This supervision is of two kinds:

- The thorough examination of statistical and accounting documents which insurance companies must provide to the Directorate-General for Insurance on a monthly, quarterly or yearly basis. This analysis uses ratios (losses/authorised capital, claims provision/premiums written, debts/liquid assets, underwriting losses, etc.) and makes it possible to check the economic, financial and liquidity situation of insurance companies. This information is indispensable for drawing up "supervisory plans" used to determine which insurance companies should be selected for on-site inspection.
- On-site inspection during which the appointed inspector makes an in-depth analysis of the economic and financial situation and the structure of the company.

In both cases the information collected is used by the supervisory authorities to specify the economic adjustments which companies must make and, if necessary, the improvements to their economic and financial solvency.

III. Measures when difficulties arise (recovery measures)

Law 33 of 2 August 1984 concerning Regulations for Private Insurance provides in Section 42 for the Ministry of the Economy and Finance to implement recovery measures in the following situations:

- Accumulated losses in excess of 25 per cent of the paid-up authorised capital of the company or mutal association fund or the permanent fund with the parent company.
- A deficit in excess of 5 per cent in the calculation of mathematical provisions, the outstanding risk or equalisation provisions, and of over 20 per cent of the unpaid claims provision.
- A deficit in excess of 10 per cent of the technical provisions.
- Inadequate solvency margins or guarantee funds.
- Liquidity problems which have resulted in late payment or non-payment.
- Problems found during supervisory inspection which jeopardise the solvency of the company, the interests of policyholders or the company's ability to meet its commitments, or inadequate or irregular accounting or management procedures which make it difficult to determine the assets and liabilities of the company.
- Liquidation of the company for one of the following reasons:
  • It is clearly unable to operate profitably.
  • Owing to management failure, it is no longer able to operate.
  • Its licence has been revoked for all authorised branches of insurance.
- If the supervisory authorities of companies located in other Member States of the European Economic Community or of insurance companies domiciled in any country of the Community which are authorised to cover risks located in Spain by free provision of services, notify the Ministry of the Economy and Finance that interim protective measures have been taken or that the licence of such a company has been revoked.

In the above cases, regardless of any penalties that may be imposed, the supervisory authorities may take the following precautionary steps as appropriate:

- A recovery plan requiring the company to specify the financial, administrative or other improvements it intends to make and to set clear goals and time limits for achieving them. The plan should not last longer than three years and the Directorate-General for Insurance must accept or reject it within a month and if need be set dates by which the company must report on the plan's progress.
- A short-term financing plan in which the company must specify the nature, amount, and scheduling of new financial resources for improving the situation. The plan should not last longer than one year, and upon accepting the plan the Directorate-General for Insurance should if need be set dates by which the company must report on the plan's progress.

- The issue of new insurance policies or acceptance of reinsurance can be suspended. This suspension will only remain in force until the recovery or financing plans mentioned above have been adopted.
- The company can be prohibited without the prior permission of the Ministry of the Economy and Finance; from making investments or payments, contracting debts, cancelling loans taken out against their contributions by members of a mutual association paying dividends, repaying loans, writing new insurance contracts or admitting new members.
- To prohibit the disposal of certain assets which will be placed in the custody of a financial manager approved by the supervisory authorities. This can be accompanied by other appropriate measures aimed at informing the public of this prohibition, such as notifying institutions holding the company's assets or securities and entry in the appropriate public registers. The decisions of the Ministry of the Economy and Finance can also be published in these registers.
- To prohibit insurance activities abroad if they are held to aggravate the situation which led to the precautionary measures.
- To convene the management bodies of the company and to appoint a proper person to chair the meeting and report back on the situation.
- To suspend the company's managers. The decision should appoint an individual or individuals to act as provisional managers, specifying whether they are to act jointly, by mutual agreement or jointly and severally.
  • To require that the necessary measures be taken to correct the adverse trend of the company's business in recent financial years.
  • To verify and guarantee within the company that precautionary measures, penalties and other provisions of the Ministry of the Economy and Finance are being enforced and intervene in the company's business if the company does not comply with those provisions.

SWEDEN

I. Introduction

The first form of legislation in Sweden regulating private insurance was to a large extent instigated by the insurance industry itself. Prior to this legislation, almost any entity could act as an insurer. The initial regulation in this area was a general law on contracts of insurance. The Insurance Contracts Act was enacted in 1927, after in-depth studies made in collaboration with other Scandinavian countries. The Act covers all direct insurance contracts to which a private insurance company is a party. Motor vehicle third-party and nuclear reactor insurance are, however, regulated by other, more specific, laws.

Further legislation regulating foreign insurance companies operating in Sweden was adopted later. These acts are still valid laws but they have been revised numerous times since their original enactments. The Insurance Business Act was enacted nationally in 1982. This act contains not only provisions relating to the supervision of the insurance industry, but also provisions corresponding to other general legislation governing commercial undertakings.

Prior to 1985, Swedish licensing authorities would not admit any new insurance company proposing to do business along traditional lines unless there was a need for more competition in that company's particular field (principle of need). After 1985, a change in the laws resulted in the licensing authorities considering only whether a new or extended licence would promote sound development of the insurance industry in general. Thus, it has become easier for new companies to obtain licences and for already existing companies to obtain extended licences. These rules apply similarly to both Swedish and foreign insurance companies. Since 1994, the requirement of soundness is restricted to the company's own activities.

The Swedish laws in general were developed in the 1970s in an attempt to increase the protection of consumers. Because these concerns for consumers carried over to the insurance sector, the Swedish Government found there was a need to improve the Insurance Contracts Act of 1927. As a result, the Government enacted the Consumer Insurance Act of 1980. This regulation applies to private contracts of non-life insurance, but is expected to be replaced in 1996 by amendments to the Insurance Contract Act of 1927.[1] Other important provisions are contained in a 1975 act on compulsory motor vehicle third-party liability insurance, which regulates the operation and supervision of insurance companies.

Significant changes have recently been enacted. An Act on Unit-Linked Insurance came into effect in 1990. The Act on Insurance Brokers was also introduced in 1990. This law allows for supervision of insurance brokers. The Supervisory Service was merged with the authority supervising banks and other credit institutions in 1991 and became the Financial Supervisory Authority (FSA). Also, since late 1990, a committee under the Ministry of Finance has reviewed certain aspects of the Insurance Business Act. The most important concern so far has been amendments needed for the implementation by 1 January 1994 of the EC directives required by the Agreement on the European Economic Agreement[2] and the implementation of the third generation EC directives on 1 July 1995.

II. Basic concepts

There are two main principles underlying the legislation governing the operation of insurance companies. The first is the principle of solvency. This is the original concern of the legislation, and requires that premiums be sufficient to cover risks insured. Second, there is the principle of equity. This requires that the cost to the policyholder be equitable and that each class of insurance pay its own way.

This mandate is particularly stringent for life insurance and other long-term personal insurance. It is less stringent for motor vehicle third-party insurance and does not apply to marine insurance, foreign non-life business of Swedish companies, or foreign companies operating in Sweden.

Swedish insurer legislation lays down a number of general principles as well as detailed provisions concerning a variety of matters with which insurance companies must comply and which at the same time will serve as a basis for supervision. For example, insurers have to produce financial statements of various kinds in prescribed forms.

The FSA has clearly defined powers to examine the accounts of a company and all relevant documents and to take measures in certain specified situations. It appoints auditors for large companies and has a special responsibility for supervising the investment of assets covering the technical reserves for life insurance and similar insurance. There are otherwise no detailed rules regarding the manner in which supervision has to be exercised. The FSA consequently has been allowed wide discretion.

III. Regulation and supervision

A. Scope and organisation of supervision

Private insurance is mainly provided by insurance companies, but there are also some friendly societies. These societies fill a certain, though diminishing, place in the sphere of life and health insurance.

They are subject to the Act on Friendly Societies of 1972 and are, as are insurance companies, under the supervision of the FSA. They are legally distinguished from insurance companies by a provision stating that they may not transact insurance business on commercial lines.

Supervision of insurance companies and of the friendly societies is the responsibility of the FSA as an independent State agency. Its work is governed only by legislation and by Government Executive Orders, which must be published. Final decisions on matters or organisation and on certain other important matters rest, however, with the Government.[3] Such matters are prepared by the FSA, which must publicly advise the Government. The Government, after obtaining the views of the FSA, resolves complaints raised against decisions made by the FSA. The Director-General has the sole right of decision in all matters which are not presented to the Board of the FSA.[4]

The Insurance Business Act does not define insurance business. Application of the legislation will determine whether a particular activity is classified as insurance. In uncertain cases it is a task for the FSA to determine whether a licence is necessary for an intended business. The FSA is authorised to prohibit unlicensed insurance activities and may impose fines against those who carry on unlicensed activities.

The Insurance Business Act does not distinguish between direct insurance and reinsurance. It does, however, make an important distinction between life insurance (including life insurance as well as annuities and pension insurance) and non-life business. There are a number of special requirements relating to life insurance.

Supervision covers all classes of direct insurance as well as reinsurance. Furthermore, it covers all private insurance companies, but only to a limited extent certain small local companies undertaking livestock insurance.

B. Foreign insurers

Supervision of foreign insurers is limited to direct insurance. No licence is needed for a foreign insurer to transact exclusively reinsurance business in Sweden, nor is there any objection if a branch of a foreign concern licensed for particular classes of direct insurance is transacting reinsurance as well. For direct insurance, the Swedish branch must be managed by a general agent as representative of the company. The branch is not regarded as an enterprise of its own, but merely as a part of the whole company.

Thus the general agent is not required to submit annual accounts of the branch business. Certain data regarding the volume of Swedish business is required merely for statistical purposes, while other data regarding life insurance is needed for ascertaining whether the assets destined for covering the mathematical reserve are of sufficient value and of prescribed standing. The FSA has the right to make unannounced inspections. For EEA insurers in Sweden home country supervision applies from 1 July 1995.

C. Supervision of business

It is incumbent upon the FSA to ensure that insurance companies remain solvent and conduct their business in accordance with Swedish laws and regulations. Supervision implies consideration of legal, financial, technical, and economic matters. Investment regulations in accordance with the third generation EC directives apply from 1 July 1995 to assets corresponding to technical provisions of life insurance as well as non-life insurance.

Solvency is monitored by means of annual and quarterly returns. The annual returns are to be sent in to the FSA no later than July-August.[5] A solvency statement according to EC rules are required annually by 15 May since 1994. Apart from EC solvency statement, the annual returns in particular are analysed. Thirteen key ratios based on the annual returns are monitored for non-life companies and a deviation from tolerance levels indicates which companies might be given priority for closer examination. These ratios are as follows:

- Increase in net premium written, between –25 per cent and +25 per cent.
- Loss ratio for own account, between 0 and 25 per cent.
- Expense ratio for own account, between 0 and 25 per cent.
- Combined ratio for own account, between 95 per cent and 105 per cent.
   a) Operating ratio for own account, between 90 per cent and 100 per cent.
- Net premium written/total premium written, between 50 per cent and 100 per cent.
- Technical result/net premium earned, between 0 and 25 per cent.
- Insurance result including allocated yield/net premium earned, between 0 and 10 per cent.
- Technical provisions for own account/surplus capital, between 0 and 350 per cent.
- Unearned premium for own account/surplus capital, between 0 and 150 per cent.
- Claims reserve for own account/surplus capital, between 0 and 200 per cent.
- Claims paid + change in claims reserve, both for own account/surplus capital, between 0 and 250 per cent.
- Net premium written/surplus capital, between 0 and 250 per cent.
- Change in surplus capital, between –20 per cent and +20 per cent.

The FSA monitors the excess of total market value of assets over policyholders' reasonable expectations on a quarterly basis. The main legal provision on the principle of equity states that the board of directors and the managing director of the company are responsible for applying it, and that is the duty of the FSA to enforce this principle. Only in the case of motor vehicle third-party insurance are there any legal provisions empowering the FSA to interfere with the setting of premium scales, as regards administration costs.

Supervision of the business of a licensed insurance company involves mainly examination of the returns which must be submitted to the FSA quarterly and annually (six or seven months after the end of the accounting year) and inspections at the insurer's place of business in order to review the whole of the company's affairs. Each major company has an auditor appointed by the FSA and each company having technical reserves for life insurance or similar insurance must register the amount and composition of the assets representing the reserves in a special record. The FSA has issued regulations concerning such registration.

D. Inspection at the place of business

At unspecified intervals, normally once every three to five years, companies may be inspected by representatives of the FSA's headquarters staff. The inspectors have access to all information available in books, correspondence minutes, contracts, internal statistical and cost analyses.

The power of the FSA to obtain information is generally unlimited, with the exception of its own capacity to use the obtained information and the moral obligation not to burden the companies in a manner that would be harmful to the interest of the policyholders.

The duty to provide information and to keep documents available for inspection also applies to rating bodies, claims settlement committees, and similar organisations of the companies.

The FSA may issue such directives concerning the conduct of an insurance company as it finds necessary. If the FSA finds that any of the following conditions are fulfilled, then it shall direct the company to take remedial measures within a specified period of time, as each case requires:

– There has been a default in complying with the law, with any regulation based on the law, with the company's articles of association, or with the technical bases, if any.
– The company's articles of association or technical bases are no longer adequate in view of the size or the character of the business.
– The assets representing the technical reserves are insufficient.
– The business in force is insufficient for such diversity of risks as is required.
– There is any other reason for serious criticism of the conduct of the company.

The FSA must report the matter to the Government if the company fails to comply with the direction within the specified time and the matters complained of are not otherwise rectified. The FSA can, after hearing any representations by the company, withdraw the company's licence to undertake insurance business.

The corresponding rules regarding foreign companies are basically the same, except that they are limited to the Swedish branch and omit the references to the articles of association and the requirement that business in force be sufficient for such diversity of risks.

The power to issue directives is rarely exercised. The fact that the FSA has this power, however, gives it more weight in negotiations.

The usual measure is to send an admonition to the companies. These admonitions are usually public documents which any newspaper or any citizen has a right to see. In a severe case, an admonition may contain an order that it be read aloud at the next company meeting (shareholder's meeting in a joint-stock company). The FSA has the right to send its own representatives to any company meeting.

Also it may order a special meeting of the board of directors to be convened and send its representatives to the meeting. Finally, it may require the board of directors to convene an extraordinary company meeting, and, if the board fails to comply, it may convene such a company meeting directly.

Almost all correspondence and other documents received by the FSA, as well as outgoing documents, are public and any person is entitled to see them. The only major exceptions from this rule concern reinsurance treaties, business secrets in companies' documents, and information pertaining to the relations between a company and individual policyholders.

IV. Financial conditions

There are no detailed rules as to the amount of a company's share capital. The minimum sum required will be settled by authorities in each individual case, taking into consideration the class of insurance, the prospective amount of business and other relevant circumstances. The share capital of a joint-stock company must be fully paid up not later than six months after its licence has been granted for registration to be made so that business can be started. Initial guarantees are required for foreign insurers.

A foreign non-EEA insurer must make a deposit at a Swedish bank before obtaining a licence. This deposit must be made on terms approved by the FSA, in securities which the FSA has accepted, and in an amount equivalent to 300 times the basic amount (approximately 1.2 million ECU for 1995).[6] A foreign non-EEA company applying for a licence must also submit the statements of account and auditors' reports for its whole business covering the last ten years or the time the company has been in existence, if less than ten years.

V. Insolvency determination

Today, the determination of insolvency is to a large extent the responsibility of the Board of Directors of each corporation, and is most clearly defined for a joint-stock insurance company. If more than two-thirds of the share capital is lost or judged to have been lost, a special balance sheet for liquidation purposes must be established. If this balance sheet verifies the presumed loss, the question of liquidation is remitted as soon as possible to the company meeting for decision. If the ordinary company meeting is too far away in time, an extraordinary company meeting is summoned. The decision to liquidate may be made at the company meeting. If so, the district court must be notified.

Another decision that may be made at the company meeting is to postpone liquidation and order management to restore the capital to half the original share capital. This respite is set to last until the ordinary company meeting of the following accounting year. If the capital is not restored to half the original after the respite, the decision to liquidate will be made by the company and the district court notified. If such a decision to liquidate is not made by the company meeting, an application for liquidation may be handed in to the district court by the Board of the company, a member of the Board, the managing director, an auditor of the company, or a shareholder. The FSA may also notify the district court of the situation. On the whole, the responsibility rests with the Board. If the regulations are not followed, some personal liability may be the result.

If the district court receives such an application for liquidation, it has the power to rule that the company must go into liquidation. It may resolve otherwise, however, if during the processing it can be verified that the capital has been restored to half the original share capital according to a balance sheet scrutinised by the auditors and accepted at the company meeting. The Court also appoints liquidators, unless this has already been done at the company meeting. If the liquidators find that the company is insolvent, they shall present the Court with a petition for bankruptcy. After this, the common bankruptcy procedure is started.

Bankruptcy is governed by the ordinary insolvency legislation and is to be registered with a district court. A petition for bankruptcy may also be handed in by a creditor. The FSA should be kept informed about a bankruptcy and has a right to appoint a representative. Such an appointment is mandatory in the case of bankruptcy of a life insurance company. There is a liquidation or winding-up procedure if the bankruptcy proceeding results in a surplus which the creditors could use to satisfy their interest.

If a mutual insurer suffers a loss in its direct non-life business that cannot be covered, it demands additional contributions from the policyholders. The next step is to reduce technical reserves and amounts paid during the year when the loss occurred. This, however, does not apply to life and health annuities arising out of accident or liability insurance because they enjoy the same protection as life business. There are no fixed rules as to when a mutual insurer must be wound up. In addition, the EC rules on solvency margin and guarantee fund apply since 1994.

VI. Suspension and cessation of business

A. Voluntary suspension

There are no provisions in Swedish legislation regarding suspension of business. If a company suspends the writing of new business in some or all classes of insurance, it is under no formal duty to report this step to the FSA, but such a report will probably be made in practice. There will be no consequences with regard to the licence. There is, however, an exception from these general rules in case of motor vehicle third-party insurance.

There are also no provisions in Swedish legislation stating directly any consequences of a voluntary cessation of a part of the business, thus the position will be mainly the same as in the case of suspension. The licence will stand, provided that the articles of association are not altered as to exclude any classes of insurance specified in the licence. If, however, the articles of association should be so altered, then the licence will lapse automatically with respect to such classes.

B. Compulsory suspension

A licence may be withdrawn by the Government if the company fails to comply with an injunction of the FSA. For a new company, the licence must be withdrawn by the Government if the company either fails to apply to the FSA for registration within six months of the Government's sanction or does not start business within three months of the registration day. It is task for the FSA to inform the Government of such matters.

Moreover, a company must be wound up if the entire insurance portfolio has been transferred to another insurer, or if the licence to undertake business has been granted for only a limited time and such time has expired without a new licence being granted. In the case of non-life classes, business may continue as necessary for a proper winding-up. Thus, current insurances will continue to be administered, *i.e.,* premiums will be collected and claims paid, until the contracts expire. A transfer of the portfolio may be arranged during the winding-up.

C. The right of appeal

The decision to withdraw a licence can only be made by the Government. Appeal can be made to the Supreme Administrative Court. The withdrawal of a licence, except where the licence is temporary or the company's articles of association have stipulated only a temporary period of business, presupposes that the FSA has notified the Government that the company has failed to comply with an injunction. Thus, the company has the opportunity to make representations publicly at both stages.

Swedish law deals with the voluntary transfer of the insurance portfolio. There are no special provisions regarding the transfer of the company as such. If a transfer comprises a company's entire insurance portfolio, it will be deemed equivalent to the transfer of the company, and will be followed by the compulsory winding-up of the company.

D. Winding-up

There is some overlap between bankruptcy under ordinary insolvency legislation and liquidation under the Insurance Business Act. The winding-up procedure is essentially the same when the bankruptcy proceeding leads to a surplus. The FSA should be kept informed about a bankruptcy and has a right to appoint a representative. In the case of a life insurance company, such an appointment is mandatory.

If a company decides to stop business voluntarily and the portfolio is not transferred to another company, the company may allow its policies to expire and decide to wind up the company afterwards, or it may decide to wind itself up immediately. In the case of the latter, business in non-life classes may continue so far as is necessary for a proper winding-up.

A voluntary winding-up requires a resolution of general meeting of the company. Even in the case of a compulsory winding-up, the law assumes that it is the company itself that has made the decision. In this case, however, only one company meeting is required. If more than two-thirds of the share capital of a joint-stock company is lost, the company must be wound up, unless the loss is made good within a certain time or a deduction of the share capital is resolved.

The procedure for winding-up is basically the same for non-insurance companies, whether the winding-up is compulsory or voluntary. One or more liquidators must be appointed at a general company meeting. The same meeting must appoint one or more liquidation auditors as well. The FSA may appoint and additional liquidator and an additional auditor in non-life insurance companies. The FSA must always appoint an additional liquidator when dealing with life insurance companies. The liquidators will be appointed by the court if the company does not do so within a certain time. The liquidators must administer, liquidate, and realise all assets and settle liabilities. As soon as this has been done they must draw up a report which, after being scrutinised by auditors, will be presented at a general company meeting.

If a foreign company winds up its branch in Sweden, it must appoint a party to represent it in relation to the policies in force in Sweden. If the company fails to meet its Swedish liabilities, the initial and additional deposits may be used. These deposits may not be released until the company has proved that all liabilities arising out of the Swedish business have been settled, unless other guarantees are substituted for the deposits and are approved.

There are special rules with regard to foreign life insurance. If the licence for this class of business is withdrawn there will be separate administratorship by the FSA. Also, in the case of the voluntary cessation of a branch business in life insurance, a separate administratorship may be prescribed by the FSA, if the representative of the company does not carry out his duty in accordance with the law, or if such a step is otherwise considered necessary in order to protect the interest of the policyholders.

E. Preferential rights

A preferential right is a right of life insurance policyholders and beneficiaries to assets covering the technical reserves. An insurer must maintain a register of assets on which there is a preferential right because there are restrictions on how such assets may be invested. These restrictions are being revised to encourage prudent portfolio management instead of dictating detailed prescriptions.

As far as domestic companies are concerned, there is a preferential right in Sweden only on the registered or recorded assets corresponding to the technical reserves for life insurance or in other insurance involving annuities arising out of accident and health insurance or motor vehicle third-party insurance. In these cases the preferential right is absolute. With regard to other classes of insurance, in general non-life classes there are no preferential right at all for the benefit of policyholders. Thus, policyholders have no greater right to the assets than other creditors.

No distinction is made between Swedish citizens and foreigners, nor between property located in Sweden or abroad. Thus all creditors, regardless of nationality, may enforce their rights on all assets of the company, including property located abroad, with only such restrictions as may be consequence of the preferential rights mentioned above or, with regard to branches of Swedish companies abroad, of preferential rights due to the legislation in the other countries.

In the case of foreign insurers, initial and additional deposits may be used only for payment of claims under insurance contracts belonging to the Swedish branch, for payment of fines, etc. These fines may be imposed on the Swedish branch or its general agent or any other representative, or, in the case of a separate administratorship for life insurance, to meet the administratorship's claim against the company.

VII. Conclusion

The regulation of the insurance industry has changed partly as a result of the Agreement on the EEA. The third generation directives were implemented by 1 July 1995. The issue whether Sweden should create a system for policyholder protection is still being discussed.

SWITZERLAND

General remarks

Supervision of private insurance in Switzerland is carried out by the Federal Department of Justice and Police and the Federal Office of Private Insurance. The Office has general supervisory authority and is empowered to take decisions except when the Supervisory Law explicitly names the Department.

Until now supervision of the solvency of insurers in Switzerland has primarily consisted of verifying the "traditional" conditions of financial soundness: equity capital at the time of starting business, security margins in premiums, adequate reinsurance, prudent choice of investments, etc.

The solvency margin laid down by the EC directives only began to be used with the entry into force of the Insurance Agreement between Switzerland and the EC on 1 January 1993 for non-life insurance and in 1994 for life insurance, when the Swisslex project adapted the country's legislation to Community Law.

I.   Regulating supervision of solvency

A.   *Life and non-life insurance companies*

1.   Equity capital

For a licence to be granted, the paid-up capital when business is begun must be between SF 600 000 and SF 10 million for non-life companies, and between SF 5 and 10 million for life insurance companies. The amount of equity capital required is determined according to the type and expected volume of insurance class operated.

To obtain a licence, the company's owners, as well as having the required capital, must constitute an organisation fund of readily convertible assets, to an amount ranging from 20 to 50 per cent of the paid-up capital, on the basis of a budget plan for the first three years of business. In the first years in business newly established insurance companies most often show a loss due to considerable organisation and starting costs (data processing, distribution network, initial commissions in life insurance). The organisation fund is intended to cover these losses so that the capital need not be used immediately.

The supervisory authority can require that the organisation fund be replenished if necessary.

The insurance company must allocate part of its yearly profit to the statutory reserve in order to create additional capital resources. This reserve is set up "according to a plan of management approved by the competent supervisory authority" (Article 671, Paragraph 6 of the Swiss Code of Obligations). As a rule, non-life insurance companies must allocate 20 per cent and life-insurance companies 10 per cent of their annual net profit to the statutory reserve until it amounts to a sum equal to 50 per cent of the company's capital.

Insurance companies' uncommitted equity capital must not be less than the solvency margin; provisions on solvency margins and guarantee funds which are in line with those of the EC have been in force since 1 January 1993 for non-life insurance, as stipulated in the Agreement on Direct Insurance Other than Life Insurance between Switzerland and the EC. Special solvency margin provisions for life insurance companies are included in the new federal legislation on direct life insurance which entered into force on 1 January 1994 in the framework of the Swisslex project.

2. Adequate reinsurance

The supervisory authorities' requirement is simply that there be adequate reinsurance of the portfolio in order to limit risks and to provide protection in the event of an unfavourable trend in claims. During the first years of business of an insurance company in particular, the joint financing of starting costs by the reinsurer also plays a role. The reinsurance policy proper, that is the choice of one or several reinsurers, the form of the reinsurance treaty (excess of loss, damage excess, etc.), the amount of the retention limit, and so on, is left to the discretion of the company concerned. However, a retention limit cannot be ruled out.

3. Technical reserves

In Switzerland technical reserves must be established on the basis of a compulsory business operation plan approved by the supervisory authority. While reserves for unexpired risks and mathematical reserves for annuity and capital payments linked to the life of one or several persons are relatively easy to determine using actuarial rules, establishing adequate reserves for outstanding claims, and especially belated claims, is much more difficult to determine for property and third party liability insurance.

In life insurance, the uncontested principle until now was that the mathematical reserve should be computed on the same basis of prudent calculation as premiums. In this way income from premiums can finance the investments which are necessary to cover the mathematical reserve over a relatively long-term average. A life insurance company could not be allowed to calculate the mathematical reserve on a lower basis than that used to calculate premiums.

4. Premium rates

In Switzerland, the supervisory authority must approve new or modified premium rates for certain risks (life and sickness insurance, third-party liability cover for lake and inland waterway vessels, mass risks incurred in other categories of compulsory insurance). The supervisory authority ensures that premium rates, established on the basis of calculations and statistics which must be submitted to it, remain within certain limits which guarantee the solvency of individual insurers while protecting policyholders against excessive rates.

5. Future policy on rates

In the near future in Switzerland, it is planned to lift not just partially but completely the requirement of prior approval of rates by the supervisory authority. This should have the effect of increasing competition, which is not undesirable. Usually, fiercer competition means tighter security margins for rates and technical reserves. Thus, the role of owners' equity in limiting risks will be much more important in the future: hence the minimum equity requirement based on type and volume of business.

6. Investments

Inasmuch as they serve to cover technical reserves (guarantee fund, tied assets), investments should be chosen in Switzerland as required by law, with due consideration for security and spread of risk, returns and liquidity requirements. Shares in foreign companies and receivables denominated in foreign currencies or imputable to foreign debtors are subject to quota. Just how meaningful such general quotas are in the light of modern portfolio management theory is another matter. On the other hand, limiting by law the proportion of securities or receivables imputable to a single enterprise or debtor, so that the insurer does not put all his eggs in one basket, seems more judicious.

Swiss insurance legislation also contains several provisions on the maximum allowable evaluation of certain investments so as to prevent misrepresentation of the solvency position through unrealistic balance-sheet assessment of assets.

B. Professional reinsurers

Foreign professional reinsurers are exempted from any supervision if reinsurance is their only business in Switzerland.

For Swiss professional reinsurers, the required capital is SF 10 million, fully paid up (an indicative order of magnitude) with an organisation fund of 20 to 50 per cent of capital. Technical reserves must be established on the basis of a compulsory business operation plan approved by the supervisory authorities.

II. Practical organisation of supervision

A. *Life and non-life insurance companies*

1. *Examination of operating plans*

When the supervisory authority initially processes the application for a licence, it examines the applicant insurance company's business operation plans, looking especially at the principles for calculating technical reserves, reinsurance regulation, plans for share participation, the general conditions of insurance and premium rates, as well as the company's organisation.

Once the licence has been granted, the supervisory authority monitors all aspects of the company's business activities on an on-going basis, examining yearly reports and conducting on-site inspections. Supervision focuses on business operations primarily from the technical, financial and legal standpoints.

2. *Examination of yearly reports*

Insurers are required to file a report every year on an official form, requiring detailed information on all aspects of business. It is primarily on this document that companies' solvency is judged. The supervisory authority monitors with special care the following factors of solvency:

- status of the statutory reserve and payments into it;
- evaluation of overall balance sheet data and analysis of the profit and loss account compared with the previous year;
- volume, appropriateness, completeness, and correct calculation of technical reserves;
- estimate of securities;
- total claims experience; levels of underwriting results and financial results;
- evaluation of operating costs and depreciation.

3. *Annual inspections of insurance companies*

For each insurance company, the supervisory authority verifies as a rule at least once a year:

- whether the amount of technical reserves (security fund, tied assets) is calculated correctly, whether it is covered by the assets allocated, and whether these assets meet the investment requirements and actually exist;
- trend of income and expenditure in relation to reinsurance, what profit and loss on risks are declared. According to the trend (for example, if reinsurance expenditures exceed reinsurance income over several years), the company in question is asked to reappraise its reinsurance treaties;
- at the time of inspection the supervisory authority also monitors policy rates and claims records; the company's accounts and organisation are also examined.

B. *Professional reinsurers*

Swiss professional reinsurers are also required to file a yearly report on an official form. On-site inspections are carried out approximately every five years. The emphasis is on the report, the accounting organisation, active and passive reinsurance, etc.

III. Measures taken in case of difficulties (recovery plan)

A. *Life and non-life insurance companies*

Swiss legislation on the supervision of private insurance provides for precautionary measures to be taken if the interests of policyholders seem to be threatened and for measures in case of the liquidation of an insurance company. The ordinary rules for the liquidation of enterprises in the Code of Obligations and the rules of the federal legislation on proceedings for debt and bankruptcy hold in principle, although there are certain modifications; in particular, the supervisory authority is competent in matters which would normally lie within the jurisdiction of the courts.

1. *Recovery measures*

If policyholders' interests are threatened, the Federal Council requires the company to take steps to correct the situation. If the insurance company does not comply with this injunction, the supervisory authority on its own initiative takes the necessary measures to protect policyholders. It can in particular transfer to another insurance company the portfolio and the security fund (or the tied assets covering the latter); or it may decide to realise, through a forced sale, the assets allocated to the security fund or the tied assets. The Federal Department of Justice and Police (''Department'') can demand a general meeting of shareholders or other body able to decide on the necessary measures for the recovery of a Swiss company. It can demand to be represented at the meeting of such a body.

2. *Breach of the rules on technical reserves*

If the company fails to comply with the provisions of insurance supervision law or with the supervisory authority's decisions on the establishment and coverage of technical reserves, the authority takes any measures it sees fit to safeguard the interests of policyholders. It can in particular prohibit the free disposal of the company's assets in Switzerland, or order that they be placed on deposit or frozen.

3. *Insufficient capital endowment or organisation fund*

If the minimum capital and organisation fund conditions are not respected, the supervisory authority requires the insurance company to put matters right by a given date. If the company disregards this injunction, the Department withdraws its licence.

4. Breach of solvency margin rules

If a Swiss insurance company's own equity no longer covers the solvency margin, the supervisory authority calls on the company to submit a recovery plan for approval. The supervisory authority can in each case lay down the recovery plan requirements and set a deadline for the plan's completion. If the insurance company fails to implement the plan in the time allotted, the Department withdraws its licence without further notice.

5. Insufficient guarantee fund

If a Swiss insurance company's owner's equity no longer covers the guarantee fund, the supervisory authority requires it to submit a short-term plan of financing for its approval. The supervisory authority can also restrict or prohibit the free disposal of the insurance company's assets and take all appropriate measures to safeguard policyholders' interests.

6. Measures by the supervisory authority

The authority may either forbid the company to surrender policies or to raise loans or advances on them (and in some cases also forbid payment of the mathematical reserve), or it may allow the company time to meet its obligations and permit policyholders to suspend premium payments.

While premium payments are suspended, insurance may not be cancelled or reduced except at the written request of the policyholder.

7. Appointment of a liquidator

If the company is liquidated, the Department can appoint a liquidator.

B. Professional reinsurers

The above measures do not apply to Swiss and foreign reinsurers (the latter are exempted from all supervision if reassurance is their only business in Switzerland). In that case adequate measures and powers are provided for, primarily in the Federal Code of Obligations and Federal law on proceedings for debts and bankruptcy. Swiss professional reinsurers are subject, in addition, to the Insurance Supervision Act (which lays down the conditions in which a licence may be withdrawn).

TURKEY

I.   Insurer solvency in Turkey

A.   *Insurer insolvency law*

Insurance sector is regulated and supervised by the Undersecretariat of Treasury and Foreign Trade[7] and inspected by the Insurance Supervisory Board.

There is a variety of legislation related to insurance companies' insolvency. The Insurance Supervision Act, amended on 15.9.1993, provides that Insurance companies may be liquidated under the Insolvency Act. This basic legislation is applicable to all insolvency procedures (corporate, limited, all kind of partnerships, real persons, etc.) and all kind of debtor or creditor relations. The Insurance Supervision Act has also important provisions related to liquidation procedures.

B.   *Determination of solvency*

According to the Insurance Supervision act, insurance companies are obligated to establish a guarantee. In non-life insurance, the guarantee is determined by the Under-secretariat in the range of 5 per cent and 20 per cent of the amount of the premiums collected. Presently this rate is 20 per cent. The guarantee to be established in life Insurance is the total amount of the amount remaining after deducting the loans made on life policies from the amount of mathematical reserve and the provisions for life out-standing claims. New companies must establish a guarantee equal to 20 per cent of their capitals as a prerequisite.

Insurance and reinsurance companies are obligated to hold their earthquake net premium retention after deducting the provision for current risks for a period of fifteen years in a fund account under the name of ''Earthquake Claims Fund''. Revenues coming from that fund must be added to the fund. Such provisions are used exclusively in meeting earthquake claims.

Securities may be deposited in cash deposit in Turkish Lira and foreign exchanges, securities issued by the State, capital market instruments defined in the Capital Market Act and determined by the Undersecretariat, and real estates.

The Undersecretariat has the authority to regulate the maximum share of an asset in the amount of guarantee and earthquake claims fund, methods and rules for valuation, depreciation margin, periods and times of establishment, blocking and release and replacement and other matters relating to the guarantee.

The Court of the Constitution has decided to abolish the Degree 510 amending Insurance Supervision Act. The decision was to be implemented after 6 months following the publishing of the decision on the Official Gazette on 22 December 1993. Therefore, the Undersecretariat have not made any regulation regarding the Degree. It is expected that within the time given by the Court there will have been made an act regarding supervising insurance companies.

Investments deposited as provisions for guarantee are blocked at the banks determined by the Undersecretariat or real estates up to 50 per cent of amount of all guarantee may be pledged over their value determined by court for their market value. Companies should establish their provisions for guarantee by the end of May.

If an insurance company fails to maintain the required guarantee on time, one month is given to maintain the guarantee. According to Article 20 of the Insurance Supervision Act if insurance or if insurance or re-insurance company could not establish the guarantee and the provisions it is required to establish or could not perform its obligations arisen from its contracts, by taking into consideration that its financial structure is weakening, after appropriate time; the Minister may require the board of directors to propose to the general assembly:

- an increase of capital or call for the payment of unpaid capital, or
- not to distribute profit, stop payment on life insurance on loan and participation and from mathematical reserves, and set aside funds for the doubtful credits, or
- dispose of participation or fixed assets partly or completely, or
- cancel the authorities to represent the company by the personnel whose acts found to be contrary to the laws and decisions, or
- change the rate and amounts and rates of the reinsurance agreements and retention shares, or
- convene the general assembly to discuss the agenda to be determined, or
- take other similar measures aimed at strengthening the financial structure.

The board of directors is obliged to take measures according to this instruction and report the measures and decision taken by it to the Undersecretariat by monthly reports.

If the board of directors fails to take partly or entirely the measures required above or the financial structure of the insurance or reinsurance company keeps weakening in spite of measures taken, the Minister may:

- appoint members to boards by removing some or all of board of directors, auditors, or by increasing the number of their members if the decision and actions taken by the board of directors have cause in weakening the financial structure of the companies;
- cancel the authority of the insurance or reinsurance company to sign new insurance contracts;
- decide to transfer the portfolio relating to one or all classes of insurance in which the company is operating together with the guarantee and funds to another company or other companies;

– cancel insurance licence if it has not been possible to strengthen the financial structure despite the measures enumerated above.

Moreover, an insurance or reinsurance company that has unsound financial position submits a plan for the restoration of a sound financial position. If the company failed in restoring sound financial position, Article 20 could be applied. However, since there is no defined and precise regulation determining financial weakness, judgement of the authorities is important in these cases. As a beginning, the Treasury has set definite and precise rules with a regulation requiring solvency margin very similar to that of EC directives.

If a company cannot meet the requirement of solvability margin, the Undersecretariat may require additional guarantee in proportion with premiums and outstanding claims.

In calculating solvency margin, provision of unearned premiums may be at least 25 per cent of premiums collected for transportation branch, 33.5 per cent of the premiums collected for the other non-life branches. However, provision for unearned premiums above minimum required level may not be accepted according to the tax laws. Mathematical provision is calculated according to actuarial principles. There are no limitations on outstanding claims in Insurance Supervision Act or tax laws. IBNR (Incurred but not reported losses) provisions may not be accepted because there are no regulation on IBNR provisions in tax laws. Securities are valued at market value. Real estate and fixed assets which may be depreciated according to tax laws are valued at purchasing value corrected by a coefficient determined by Ministry of Finance according to the inflation rate. Real estate and fixed assets which may not be depreciated according to tax laws are valued at purchasing value. Receivables and debts are not discounted but nominal values are taken. Regarding high inflation rates, high premium receivables and high rate of investment in real estate in Turkey, taking purchasing value of real assets and nominal value of receivables and debts can destroy solvability margin substantially.

By the Decree 510 some regulation put on application to solve the high premium receivables problem. Insurance licence of an insurance company failing to cancel the authority to issue policy of the agencies who have failed to transfer in time the premiums collected by them may be cancelled. The premiums collected by agencies must be transferred to insurance companies in 10 days. That time was one month under the Decree 510. Insurance companies are obligated to make provisions for premium receivables which is thought risky and could not be collected within six months. The procedures and rules for such provision are to be set forth by the Undersecretariat. Under the Decree 510 insurance companies are obligated to show the amount and due dates in the policies.

Insurance and reinsurance companies have to set aside 5 per cent of their profits as "Extra-ordinary Claims Fund" until it reaches the amount of their paid capital. This fund may be used only to meet technical losses.

A new insurance and reinsurance company should have minimum paid capital of 50 billion Turkish Liras to be able to get insurance licence. Companies which already have insurance licence have to increase their paid in capital to the minimum level in 3 years. The Ministry is authorised to increase the minimum amount of paid in capital in proportion with the rate of increase of the wholesales price index of State Statistics institute.

It can be criticised that the system based on guarantee can create some problems of liquidity in particular ability to pay claims. However, the guarantee system was installed by the Act when rates were set by the authorities and there were no competition. Companies audited by the Insurance Auditors Board and controlled by Milli Reasürans T.A.S., the reinsurance company to which insurance companies were required to cede about 25 per cent of premiums ceded. Milli Re has authority to inspect pricing and claims policy of Insurance companies which was very effective when insurance companies had to cede premiums on quote par to Milli Re and fixed rates was on application.[8] Also, retention tables should be approved by the authorities.

There was not much need to audit companies financially because of such a conservative system. However, this has prevented development and growth of sector. After 1990, a restructuring and liberalisation have taken place. Tariffs, except compulsory insurance, have been determined by the companies since 1990. After the free fate system, sectors have faced a competitive era. and existing business have been allowed. Financial auditing has become more important. However, because of guarantee system, financial auditing is still not so vital.

Because of high competitive and chaotic environment due to the free tariff system, insufficient and underdeveloped infrastructure of the sector and auditing, guarantee system cannot be abolished in short run but it could be abolished gradually in the long run.

C. Insolvency determination

There are two kinds in liquidating any insolvent company that is known as winding-up: Compulsory and voluntary.

1. Compulsory liquidation

The most common ground on which a company is compulsory wound up it that it is unable to pay its debts. However compulsory liquidation may be initiated on the basis of a court determination that liquidation is just and equitable.

Companies whose licence is cancelled, declared bankrupt or ceased operation for other reasons are wound up according to the provisions of the relevant laws being subject to the Undersecretariat's control.

If the winding-up order is made, the Liquidation Office administers the winding-up until first creditors' meeting. If creditors who have 1/4 of debts of the company do not participate in the meeting and if the number of them is less than five, or if creditors who have 1/2 of debts of the company do not participate, the Liquidation Office administer all liquidation process. In the first creditors meeting 3 persons are elected as administrator of the liquidation commission. Two of the administrators are elected by and represent creditors who have majority of the company's debts and the third person is elected by and represents majority of the creditors. The Liquidation Office also supervises the liquidation commission and has right to want the administrators withdraw. For an insolvent insurance company the Undersecretariat has that right as well. The Liquidation Office is tied to Ministry of Justice and complaints about the office can be made to the court.

2. *Voluntary liquidation*

Article 324 of the Commercial Act requires that the board of directors of a company which lost its half paid capital report the financial position of the company to the stockholders. And if the company lost more than $2/3$ of the paid capital, the stockholders should raise capital, at least, to $1/3$ of the paid capital or should dissolve the company by appoint one or more liquidates to winding-up the company's affairs and distributing its assets. Creditors should accept discounted payment made by the company before due date. If debts of the company are more than the company's assets, the board of directors must voluntarily request liquidation of the company from the commercial court. Creditors can request liquidation of the company if they cannot get guarantee for their receivables. (Article 436.)

If an insurance or reinsurance company desired to stop operating and wind up its affairs after getting the Ministry's permission, the company is obligated to make public its decision through at least two newspapers, and to give notice to its creditors and deposits the necessary guarantee.

D. *Rehabilitation versus liquidation*

If the survival of the company as a going concern might be assured or a more advantageous realisation of assets achieved than in liquidation, the court may enter an Administrator Order or Voluntary Arrangements may be made. All creditors have the right to object the court decision.

Also, if a company cannot meet its liabilities as they fall due, the parties in control of the company, who may be the directors, provisional liquidators, or creditors, draw up a scheme under which the creditors agree to adopt a proportion of their outstanding debt, receiving it earlier and possibly receiving more than they might expect under a liquidation of the company. Such an arrangement is basically an agreement or a moratorium between a company and its creditors that has a binding effect once approved by the court. However, such arrangements are far slower and more cumbersome than voluntary arrangements. The scheme must be approved by a $2/3$ in number and by $2/3$ in value of each class of creditors but credits have guarantee.

However such an application is almost impossible for an insurance company because of provisions of the Insurance Supervisory act.

E. *Enhancement of the estate*

Under the Insolvency Act, a pre-liquidation transfer of assets not for adequate value is avoidable by the liquidation if the transaction occurred in the two years prior to the insolvency. A preference is also avoidable by the liquidator if it took place during the one year period prior to insolvency, although this time period can be extended to two years if the person receiving the alleged preference was an insider, that is one connected to the insolvent insurer. With respect to a preference, some proof must be shown that the insolvent company was influenced in the transaction by a desire to place the creditor in a better position than other creditors in the event of a subsequent liquidation and that the company was insolvent at the time of the transaction.

Interest charging for debts but secured debts (including claims related to life insurance), also, expired after beginning of the liquidation.

Under the Insolvency act, funds distributed through creditors as follows:

- First, secured creditors, *i.e.,* creditors secured under a fixed charge such as a mortgagee with a mortgage on real property. Guarantee funds related to premiums and mathematical reserves can be used only for claims to insured; receivables of the insured are counted as secured credits.
- Second, preferential creditors after receivables of the insolvency commission and duties risen sale of assets. Priority of preferential creditors before insureds as follows: first; unpaid wages and salaries one year prior to the liquidation and seniority indemnities[9] of employee. Second; debts to employee assistance and support funds, foundations and associations.
- Third, claims to insureds and agents' receivables related to agency contract or function prior to the liquidation.

There are no regulations but it is expected that insureds have the utmost priority over payments made by reinsurers.

An insured has the right to cancel the insurance policy and get money back for unexplored period of the insurance policy.

If all claims to insured are paid, the Undersecretariat will be free to deal with blocked securities and will release pledge on real estate. After that, debts to the other creditors can be paid.

At last, if directors found being guilty because of improper financial condition of the company, they would be responsible with their personal assets.

UNITED KINGDOM

I. Regulations concerning the supervision of solvency

The Insurance Companies Act 1982 gives the Secretary of State for Trade and Industry Powers to authorise and supervise insurance companies writing business in the United Kingdom. The Act provides the main legislative framework within which Insurance Division of the Department of Trade and Industry (DTI) works. It is supplemented by regulations which provide greater detail and which, although still subject to Parliamentary scrutiny, are easier to amend than the Act itself. There will be considerable amendment of the regulations in the next few months to bring them into compliance with the EC Third Directives which come into force in July 1994.

The Act requires companies to obtain authority from the Secretary of State before they may write insurance: he has the power to prevent anyone managing or controlling an insurance company trading in the UK if they appear to him not to be "fit and proper".

The act establishes two critical requirements:

- Insurance companies have to maintain a prescribed solvency margin of assets (on a common EC definition) in excess of their liabilities, prudently assessed.
- Detailed financial information must be made regularly available to the DTI and to the public.

The Act also gives the Secretary of State power to intervene in policyholders' interests when it is appropriate. These intervention powers are discussed in Section III below.

A guiding principle of the legislation is to allow insurance companies the maximum freedom of operation whilst ensuring that their activities are publicly reported. Publicity is achieved by making publicly available the detailed audited annual returns which companies have to provide for the Secretary of State; these are separate and additional to the shareholders' (or members') annual report and accounts, which are often less detailed and not, until the implementation of the EC Insurance Accounts Directive in 1995, produced in a standard format. Thus, policyholders, competitors, brokers, market analysts and journalists have access to the information that the annual returns contain. This has resulted in a growing number of comparative analyses of data and an increasing market in insurance information – producing a more informed market in insurance products.

Amongst many other things, the regulations prescribe the form in which the returns should be made to DTI and the prudent asset valuation methods which must be used in the returns. They also provide for significant shareholders, directors and managers to be notified to the DTI so that their fitness can be considered. For life companies the legislation requires the appointment of an actuary who is responsible for determining each year the company's long term liabilities based on prescribed valuation rules. The Appointed Actuary's responsibilities however go far wider than the legislative requirement as he is bound by professional guidance notes to be satisfied that, should he carry out a valuation of the company's liabilities at any time, the financial position of the company would be satisfactory.

UK reinsurers are supervised in the same way as direct insurers, unlike in many other countries.

A separate statute, the Policyholders' Protection Act 1975, provides for some, mainly private, policyholders to benefit from a protection scheme if their insurers fail. Payments are funded by a levy on authorised insurance companies.

Special arrangements apply to Lloyds's which largely regulates itself under the Lloyd's Acts 1871 and 1982. However, Lloyd's as a whole is required to report its solvency to the DTI annually on a comparable basis to insurance companies and its auditor must certify that each underwriter at Lloyd's is solvent.

II. The practical organisation of supervision

All insurance supervision is carried out on behalf of, and in the name of, the Secretary of State by officials in the Insurance Division of the Department of Trade and Industry. Ministers are consulted on, or notified about, policy issues and developments on significant cases and they are answerable to Parliament on any issue which may be raised there, but they do not become involved in the day-to-day supervision.

Insurance Division, unlike the supervisors in some other countries, is responsible both for the development of policy and regulations as well as direct supervision.

The Division employs around 100 staff, most of whom are permanent civil servants. A small but increasing number are professionals with accountancy, actuarial and insurance market place experience, who are mainly engaged as managers of teams of supervisors who each have a set portfolio of companies. A separate group within Insurance Division concentrate on new authorisations.

Additional help for the Division comes from four full-time members of the DTI's Solicitor's Department; and at the Government Actuary's Department 15 qualified actuaries provide expert advice to the Division especially on the solvency of life companies, but increasingly also on general business.

Some 80 per cent of the Division's cost are recovered from insurers through annual fees paid when returns are deposited. The size of the fee depends on the insurer's premium income. The insurance industry has a vested interest in the effectiveness of insurance supervision in the United Kingdom because companies have to contribute towards compensation in the event of insolvency.

Supervision is exercised principally through examination of annual returns; more extensive reporting requirements for new companies, where there has been change of control or the company is causing concern; and by personal contact with the company management, including visits to companies.

A. Examination of returns

An important feature of the returns is that they have to be audited. The auditor has to satisfy himself that acceptable accounting and control systems are in place and that the assets are valued in accordance with the regulations. This means that the DTI does not itself need to check on the spot in the company that the records are adequate or that the assets truly exist.

In addition, although only for life companies, the Appointed Actuary of the company is under a professional obligation which provides comfort about the reliance which may be put on the return.

Returns from life companies and the life funds of composites are examined by the Government Actuary's Department, while general business returns are examined by supervisors in Insurance Division, at least in the first instance.

For general business returns the supervisors examine each of the returns closely on receipt. The first step is to look for early warning of problems using ratio tests covering solvency, profitability, growth rate, liquidity etc. and looking at other key risk areas such as reinsurance protection and source of additional capital. If necessary, more detailed work on the adequacy of reserving is done using computer support, or the company is referred to an actuary at GAD for detailed examination.

A similar process of a quick initial review to determine priorities followed up by more detailed examination as needed is also followed at GAD for life returns.

Concerns and queries arising out of the returns are followed up with companies and this process often leads to discussion of their problems and future plans.

B. More extensive reporting requirements

In order to anticipate and, if possible, to prevent solvency problems arising, it is quite normal practice to require potentially vulnerable companies to provide additional information which, unlike the annual returns, is confidential between the company and the DTI. Such requirements are almost always imposed on authorisation and following a change of control and can be retained for up to 10 years. In addition, similar requirements are imposed on companies which appear to be financially weak. The additional information would generally include quarterly financial reporting; notification of any investments in, or transactions, with connected parties; actuarial reports (additional to those standard ones required from life companies); the provision of, and notification of any changes to, the business plan; and other requests specifically designed for the individual company.

C. *Personal contact*

In addition to meetings with companies which are seeking DTI approval when required by the legislation or where there are financial or other difficulties, Insurance Division and GAD make regular visits to companies. These are not detailed inspections but, rather, opportunities to meet the senior management to form a view about their quality and to discuss their future plans. The annual returns are inevitably backward-looking and out of date by the time that they arrive. The visits therefore help to keep up to date with developments in the market. Also by establishing personal contact the visits help to encourage management to let their supervisor know about plans and problems of concern to the Division at an early stage which will allow the supervisor to influence how they are handled.

III. Recovery measures when difficulties arise

Effective supervision, although in a free market it can never prevent all companies getting into difficulties, should at least allow time for steps to be taken to avoid problems becoming critical to the solvency of insurers. The approach described above is designed to allow this to happen without requiring the formal use of the intervention powers prescribed in the legislation. Much of the DTI's insurance supervision is conducted in this flexible and informal way. Nevertheless, this approach is backed up by a wide range of intervention powers which are defined quite specifically in the legislation, together with the grounds for their possible use.

The main grounds for the use of formal powers are:

– That the company has failed to satisfy an obligation under the Insurance Companies Act, for example in the case of financial difficulties, the failure to maintain the required minimum margin of solvency.
– That it appears that the company has furnished the Secretary of State with misleading or inaccurate information *e.g.* have deliberately concealed a weak financial position.
– That reinsurance is inadequate.
– That controllers, managers or directors are unfit.

However, intervention powers that involve taking control over a company's assets can only be used if in addition:

– the company's authorisation to write new business has been withdrawn;
– its solvency margin is seriously eroded well below the required minimum;
– its liabilities have not been calculated according to the regulations.

The requirement for specific grounds is designed to prevent arbitrary misuse of the powers but does occasionally cause difficulties where, for example, a company has met the minimum EC solvency margin but is, nevertheless, in the supervisor's views inadequately capitalised.

The most common ground, or trigger, for intervention when a company encounters financial difficulties is its failure to maintain the required minimum margin of solvency.

This may become apparent at any point, not simply when the annual return is submitted. The DTI will then require a plan for the restoration of a sound financial position. In some cases this can be achieved simply by the injection of additional capital from a parent. Often the solution is less straightforward, and the DTI will work with the company to develop a plan which may entail sale of parts of the business, withdrawal from certain lines of business, restriction of premium income or complete cessation of writing of new business.

However, a complete stop can destroy the goodwill in the business which reduces the amounts for which parts or all of the business or its assets can be sold. This in turn jeopardises the interests of existing policyholders. In taking intervention action the DTI has to have regard to the classic regulator's dilemma – intervention that turned out to be premature could damage the interests of existing policyholders, while intervention too late can permit more damage in the interim, particularly for new policyholders.

Once a plan is agreed by the DTI the company is required to implement it and the DTI will impose requirements such as those mentioned in II.*B.* above to assist it in monitoring progress.

Even if a company ceases to write any new business and has its authorisation to write withdrawn it continues to remain subject to DTI's financial supervision until all existing obligations to policyholders are met, which may take many years. During this period it can become apparent that the company will fail to complete a solvent run off, perhaps because of unanticipated claims, or because assets, such as reinsurance recoveries, prove uncollectable. In such cases, the DTI would intervene again to ensure that the directors are aware of their responsibilities not to continue to trading while insolvent. It would be an unfair preference to pay policyholders' current claims in full when it is clear that claims which fall due at a later date cannot be met. The DTI recognises, however, that it is rarely in the interest of policyholders for an insurance company to be wound up, largely because of the costs and time involved in liquidation. The legislation provides in any event for every effort to be made to transfer life business to another insurer. Similar efforts would be made for a general business insurer, but, if this fails, it is becoming the practice to try to arrange a scheme of arrangement with creditors, sanctioned by the Courts, which allows the insurer to continue to pay a conservative percentage of claims as they fall due, to ensure that all policyholders, regardless of when their claims mature, receive the same proportionate payout. The percentage can be increased or decreased as further information on the company position emerges.

If recovery measures fail, the DTI does have powers, in the last resort, to petition the Court for company to be wound up. Even at this point private policyholders remain protected because their policies will either be transferred, or their claims met through the Policyholders' Protection Board levy.

The legislation provides other intervention powers, for example, for when a senior figure appears not be fit and proper for their position. The appointment of directors, controllers and managers must be notified to Insurance Division, and if a person is considered unfit for a post, on appointment or subsequently, there are statutory procedures for objection. After hearing representations, the Division can issue a formal notice of objection and then, if the company refuses to take appropriate action, can prevent the company from taking on new business. The threat of such drastic action is usually quite sufficient to ensure that the unfit person is removed. The appointed actuary must be notified to DTI and is subject to the disciplinary procedures of the actuarial profession.

UNITED STATES

Introduction

The primary objectives of insurance regulation in the United States are to protect the interests of policyholders, assure insurance company solvency and assure that rates are not inadequate, excessive, or unfairly discriminatory. Of these objectives, the one that is perhaps most fundamental to protecting consumers is solvency regulation.

Individual states are responsible for regulating the insurance business within their own jurisdictions. To facilitate this state regulation of insurance, each state maintains its own insurance department. Each of these departments is organised under the supervision of a commissioner (or director or superintendent) who is either appointed or elected.

I.   Basic components of solvency regulation

A.   *Regulatory requirements*

Capital and surplus provide a cushion against unexpected increases in liabilities and decreases in the value of assets, and is intended to fund the costs of a rehabilitation or liquidation of an insurer with minimal losses to policyholders and claimants. States require insurers to have a certain amount of capital and surplus to establish and continue operations. Regulators may seize a company if they can show that it will be unable to meet its obligations to policyholders.

Current fixed minimum capital and surplus standards typically range in the area of US$2 million for a multi-line insurer. However, regulators are increasingly critical of fixed-capital standards because they are: 1) unrelated to risk; 2) too low for many insurers; and 3) provide an insufficient basis for timely regulatory action against failing companies. Because of these limitations of fixed minimum capital standards, the NAIC has adopted RBC formulas for life/health and for property/casualty companies, and a model law prescribing regulatory action based upon the results of those formulas. The stated objectives of the NAIC RBC requirements are to provide a standard of capital adequacy that: 1) is related to risk; 2) raises the safety net for insurers; 3) is uniform among states; and 4) provides authority for regulatory action when actual capital falls below the standard.

The NAIC's life/health RBC formula encompasses four major categories of risk: 1) asset risk; 2) insurance or pricing risk; 3) interest rate risk; and 4) business risk. The risks addressed by the NAIC's property/casualty formula include: 1) asset risk; 2) credit risk (uncollectible reinsurance and other receivables); 3) underwriting (pricing and reserve) risk; and 4) off-balance sheet risk (*e.g.*, guarantees of parent obligations, excessive growth).

Under the model act, certain company and regulatory actions are required if a company's total adjusted capital falls below its calculated RBC level. The act establishes four levels of company and regulatory action, with more severe action required at lower levels.

B. Asset valuation reserve/Interest maintenance reserve

Another important development in regulatory requirements for life/health insurance companies is the institution of the Asset Valuation Reserve (AVR) and the Interest Maintenance Reserve (IMR). The AVR establishes reserve requirements for all major asset classes including securities, real estate, and mortgage loans. The IMR requires insurers to amortise interest-related gains and losses over the remaining life of the disposed asset.

Other statutes and regulations pertain to insurers' investment practices and various aspects of their operations. Most states require insurers' investments to be diversified and many have placed limits on the amount of lower quality bonds that insurers can invest in. Holding company laws control transactions between affiliated companies, including the payment of dividends from a subsidiary to a parent. Insurers are prohibited from improper delegation of authority to managing general agents with respect to underwriting and paying claims.

States require insurers to maintain records and file financial statements with regulators in accordance with statutory accounting practices (SAP). Under SAP, assets are valued conservatively and certain non-liquid assets, *e.g.* furniture and fixtures, are not admitted in the calculation of an insurer's surplus.

C. Solvency monitoring/Surveillance

The fundamental objective of solvency monitoring is to ensure that insurance companies meet regulatory standards and to alert regulators if actions need to be taken to protect policyholders. To accomplish this task, states require insurers to file annual and quarterly financial statements and to submit themselves to financial examinations.

States have expanded financial reporting requirements to provide more detailed and accurate financial information. Schedules dealing with reinsurance, bonds, real estate and mortgage loan investments, and loss reserves have been enhanced. Statements of actuarial opinion, asset adequacy analysis and independent audit requirements also have been instituted.

States generally will prioritise the review of their domiciliary companies and any companies that require expedited scrutiny. Most departments use some system of financial ratios or other tools to screen and prioritise insurers for analysis. Regulators also use

NAIC financial information systems including the Insurance Regulatory Information System (IRIS) which includes the Financial Analysis and Surveillance Tracking (FAST) system, and other reports.

State insurance departments and the NAIC review the annual and quarterly financial statements through a variety of systems. Insurers that appear to be healthy based on their financial results receive no further scrutiny, with the exception of their regular examination, unless other information indicates a need for further investigation. Insurers with anomalous results or that have been the subject of previous attention receive further scrutiny and analysis. For such an insurer, regulators will perform a more detailed analysis and likely request additional information and explanations from the insurer.

The domiciliary state is relied upon as the primary solvency regulator. Other states in which a company is licensed will perform some monitoring and take action if necessary. The NAIC facilitates co-ordination and communication among state regulators concerning insurers' financial condition through its information network, financial analysis systems and committee structure.

D. Financial reporting

The annual statement has evolved considerably since its introduction by the NAIC in 1875. The current statement is an extensive document containing a balance sheet and income statement as well as a number of supporting exhibits and schedules. The most significant exhibits/schedules in the annual statement include: assets; liabilities and surplus; summary of operations (life/health only); statement of income (property/casualty only); cash flow; underwriting and investment exhibit (property/casualty only) and similar investment exhibits in the life/health statement; analysis of assets; real estate; mortgages; other long-term investments; collateral loans; bonds and stocks; Asset Valuation/Interest Maintenance Reserves (life/health only); short-term investments; financial Options; Reinsurance; Transactions with Affiliates; General Interrogatories; notes to the financial statement; and information regarding management and directors. Most insurers also are required to file quarterly statements that contain key information on assets and liabilities, income, changes in investment holdings, premiums written, losses and reserves. The quarterly statements are an important regulatory tool for detecting trends in a company's financial condition.

E. Solvency screening/Analysis systems

1. Insurance Regulatory Information System (IRIS)

The NAIC's IRIS has served as a baseline solvency screening system for the NAIC and state regulators since the mid-1970s, and is designed to help regulators prioritise insurers for detailed financial analysis. The first phase of IRIS involves calculating a series of financial ratios for each insurer based on its annual statement data. An experienced team of examiners and analysts then reviews these financial ratio results along with selected insurers' annual statements and categorises insurers by regulatory priority.

2. Financial Analysis and Solvency Tracking (FAST) System

Recently, the NAIC expanded IRIS to encompass a new solvency screening model and analytical process to facilitate peer review of domiciliary regulation of "nationally significant" insurers. The objective of the NAIC's peer review process, as exercised throughout its Financial Analysis Working Group (FAWG), is to ensure that domiciliary regulators are taking effective action with respect to "nationally significant" insurers that are in financial difficulty.

The NAIC's Financial Analysis Division subjects these insurers' financial statements to a computerised analytical routine, FAST, which prioritises companies for further analysis. FAWG reviews this analysis and identifies those insurers that it will subject to review. For those insurers, FAWG queries the domiciliary state on various aspects of the insurers' financial condition and regulatory actions with respect to those insurers. If FAWG determines that the domiciliaryregulator has taken the appropriate actions then FAWG may close the file or continue to monitor the company. If FAWG determines that further measures are desirable, it will recommend the appropriate corrective action to the domiciliary state. If the domiciliary regulator fails to follow FAWG's recommendation, FAWG will alert other states accordingly and co-ordinate their actions against the troubled company.

The NAIC makes available the IRIS/FAST ratios to all state regulators over the NAIC's computer network. State regulators also have access to a CD-ROM system, the Financial Analyst Work-bench, which includes the IRIS/FAST ratios as well as several other valuable databases relating to insurance companies including investment analyses, SEC filings, corporate reports, and news articles. This provides a comprehensive tool kit for regulatory solvency analysis and the evidence suggests that states are making extensive use of it.

3. Examinations

Examinations have been a mainstay of insurer solvency monitoring. The basic purposes of an examination system are: 1) to detect as early as possible those insurers in financial trouble and/or engaging in unlawful and improper activities; and 2) to develop the information needed for appropriate regulatory action.

The scope of a comprehensive examination encompasses a number or areas, including an insurer's: management and control; plan of operation; corporate records; accounts and records; financial statements; business in force; mortality and loss experience; reserves; quality of assets, and reinsurance. The NAIC encourages the use of "association" or "zone" examinations in which states from each region participate.

One important component of improved examination procedures is the use of automated examinations. The NAIC has helped to develop automated exam systems and provides consulting support to assist state examiners in the pre-examination and on-site phases. The Examination Jumpstart system generates a series of analytical reports from the NAIC's database that allow the supervising examiner to pin-point problem areas and allocate resources accordingly before going on-site. The system also performs many routine, time-consuming tasks that the examiner would otherwise perform at the company. Special audit software is used at the company to retrieve, check and analyse information from its electronic files.

4. Others Sources of Information

Regulators are continually looking for other sources of information to supplement standard financial reporting in order to detect earlier problems that may jeopardise a company's long-term viability. These sources include SEC filings, corporate reports, CPA audits, actuarial opinions, market conduct reports, consumer complaints, rating agencies, contacts from agents and insurers, and business media.

F. Actions against troubled companies

The objective of a regulatory solvency monitoring system is to identify, in a timely manner, insurers in need of regulatory attention in order to prevent or minimise losses due to insolvencies and to provide protection for the insurance consumer. Actions to prevent a financially troubled insurer from becoming insolvent include hearings/conferences, corrective plans, restrictions on activities, notices of impairment, cease and desist orders, and supervision. If preventive regulatory actions are unsuccessful and an insurer becomes severely impaired or insolvent, then a state will institute more formal delinquency proceedings, such as conservation, seizure of assets, rehabilitation, liquidation and dissolution.

State guaranty associations have been established to protect, within statutory limits, policyholders, claimants, and beneficiaries against financial losses due to insurer insolvencies. Guaranty funds are financed by assessments on licensed insurers' premiums written in covered lines of business in that state, subject to an annual cap. Assessments generally are made after an insolvency occurs to cover the claims of the insolvent insurer.

II. State insurance department resources

Each insurance department is under the supervision of an official who is either appointed or elected. In 1992, the size of departments' staffs varied from 24 to 1 390 with a total combined staff of 9 691 in addition to 1 836 contract staff. Similarly, for fiscal year 1994, state department budgets range from US$1 239 396 to US$79 298 000, with a total combined budget of approximately US$592 million.

Despite tight fiscal constraints overall, the states have significantly increased the resources devoted to insurance regulation in recent years. From 1987 to 1994, funding for state insurance departments increased by 86.7 per cent, three and a half times the pace of inflation over this period. The increase in financial staff and computers has allowed regulators to improve the effectiveness and timeliness of solvency monitoring activities.

III. The role of the National Association of Insurance Commissioners (NAIC)

The NAIC is an organisation of the chief insurance regulatory officials of the 50 states, the District of Columbia, and the four territories. It was established in 1871 to co-ordinate the supervision of interstate companies within a state regulatory framework. The NAIC co-ordinates and assists state solvency efforts in a number of ways, including: 1) maintaining an extensive insurance database and computer network linking all insurance departments; 2) analysing and informing regulators as to the financial condition of insurance companies; 3) co-ordinating examinations and regulatory actions with respect to troubled companies; 4) establishing and certifying states' compliance with minimum financial regulation standards; 5) providing financial, reinsurance, actuarial, legal, computer and economic expertise to insurance departments; 6) valuing securities held by insurers; 7) analysing and listing non-admitted alien insurers; 8) developing uniform statutory financial statements and accounting rules for insurers; 9) conducting education and training programs for insurance department staff; 10) developing model laws and co-ordinating regulatory policy on significant insurance issues; and 11) conducting research and providing information on insurance and its regulation to regulators, state legislators, Congress, US government agencies, insurance regulators in other countries, and the general public. These activities facilitate state regulators' oversight of a complex industry extending across state and national boundaries.

A. *Databases and information systems*

The NAIC has amassed an extensive financial database on insurance companies accessible to state insurance departments and other users through a computer information network. The NAIC database contains five years of detailed annual and quarterly financial information on-line for approximately 5 000 insurance companies as well as data archived back to the mid-1970s.

The NAIC database serves as the core of the solvency surveillance and other analysis activities of state insurance regulators and the NAIC. State regulators and NAIC staff access the database through a variety of application systems that allow them to review data on specific companies, generate "canned" reports on a group of companies, or generate custom reports to suit their specific needs. More than 5 000 insurance department users have direct access to the NAIC system. Regulators also have access to the NAIC database on CD-ROM and other media. In addition, the NAIC provides its insurance database to federal agencies, academics, rating organisations, and various other users.

The NAIC maintains a number of other databases which state regulators and NAIC staff use for financial analysis and other regulatory functions. The Alien Reporting Information System (ARIS) provides financial reports that show reinsurance ceded to domestic or alien reinsurers. The on-line Valuation of Securities (VOS) system provides a complete VOS manual, listing securities held by insurers, along with historical data beginning with 1989.

There are two special databases containing information on regulatory actions against insurers and agents – the Regulatory Information Retrieval System (RIRS) – and information on entities of regulatory concern – the Special Activities Database (SAD). RIRS and SAD enhance regulators' ability to share information on individuals or companies suspected of illegal or questionable activities and prevent their infiltration into new areas. State regulators and NAIC staff also use an electronic mail system on the NAIC's computer network to communicate and co-ordinate with respect to examinations, regulatory actions, troubled companies, entities of regulatory concern, and a variety of other matters.

B. Financial analysis and solvency monitoring

The NAIC serves an important co-ordinating function in the event that multi-state insurance companies experience financial difficulty, primarily through computerised monitoring systems (such as IRIS and FAST, discussed above) as well as in-house financial analysis of insurance companies, the results of which are disseminated to regulators.

C. Financial regulation standards and accreditation programme

In June 1989, the NAIC adopted the Financial Regulation Standards, which establish baseline requirements for state solvency regulation in three area: 1) laws and regulations; 2) regulatory practices and procedures; and 3) organisational and personnel practices. To provide guidance to the states regarding the minimum standards and an incentive to put them in place, the NAIC adopted a formal certification programme in June 1990. Under this plan, an independent review team reviews each insurance department's compliance with the NAIC's Financial Regulation Standards. All states have enacted legislation designed to achieve compliance with the NAIC standards, and insurance department budgets and staffing have increased rapidly. As of September 1, 1994, 36 states were accredited under the NAIC standards.

D. Other NAIC functions

The NAIC's Securities Valuation Office (SVO) determines uniform accounting values of insurers' securities investments that include government, municipal and corporate bonds, and common and preferred stocks.

The Non-Admitted Insurers Information Office (NAIIO) maintains a Quarterly Listing of Alien Insurers which states may use to determine surplus lines carriers eligible or approved to operate in their jurisdiction. Market conduct support activities also have expanded significantly at the NAIC to assist the states in their responsibilities in this area. In addition to maintaining the RIRS and SAD systems, the NAIC has developed a nationwide complaint database, a database on insurance company officers and directors and an overall system for tracking basic profile data on entities involved in the insurance business. The NAIC also provides important education, training, and research services to state insurance departments and their staffs.

Notes and References

1. Similar acts are being discussed for the field of life insurance contracts.
2. The EEA Treaty is a corporate agreement between some of the EFTA countries which are not members of the European Community (EC) and the EC. It gives the Scandinavian countries some of the benefits of being member nations of the EC.
3. The term ''Government'' refers to the Board of Ministers established by the leaders of the party of coalition of parties which received the majority of votes in the parliamentary election. The Board receives its power from the Swedish Constitution.
4. There are no advisory bodies, but the FSA has the liberty to call in independent experts when it so desires. This has been done occasionally in the past.
5. An acceleration of this process is currently being discussed.
6. The basic amount is a unit related to inflation and consumer prices. For 1995, 300 times the basic amount equals SKr 10 710 000.
7. In 1988, the Undersecretariat took responsibility of regulation of Sector from the Ministry of Industry and Trade.
8. According to the Decree which came into force in 1992, insurance companies which have retention ratio over 75 per cent are not obligated to cede premiums to Milli Re.
9. Employees get seniority payments, which equal their gross wages multiplied by 2 and number of years worked, if they are quitted by the employer.

MAIN SALES OUTLETS OF OECD PUBLICATIONS
PRINCIPAUX POINTS DE VENTE DES PUBLICATIONS DE L'OCDE

ARGENTINA – ARGENTINE
Carlos Hirsch S.R.L.
Galería Güemes, Florida 165, 4° Piso
1333 Buenos Aires   Tel. (1) 331.1787 y 331.2391
                                 Telefax: (1) 331.1787

AUSTRALIA – AUSTRALIE
D.A. Information Services
648 Whitehorse Road, P.O.B 163
Mitcham, Victoria 3132   Tel. (03) 873.4411
                                 Telefax: (03) 873.5679

AUSTRIA – AUTRICHE
Gerold & Co.
Graben 31
Wien I   Tel. (0222) 533.50.14
                                 Telefax: (0222) 512.47.31.29

BELGIUM – BELGIQUE
Jean De Lannoy
Avenue du Roi 202 Koningslaan
B-1060 Bruxelles   Tel. (02) 538.51.69/538.08.41
                                 Telefax: (02) 538.08.41

CANADA
Renouf Publishing Company Ltd.
1294 Algoma Road
Ottawa, ON K1B 3W8   Tel. (613) 741.4333
                                 Telefax: (613) 741.5439
Stores:
61 Sparks Street
Ottawa, ON K1P 5R1   Tel. (613) 238.8985
211 Yonge Street
Toronto, ON M5B 1M4   Tel. (416) 363.3171
                                 Telefax: (416)363.59.63

Les Éditions La Liberté Inc.
3020 Chemin Sainte-Foy
Sainte-Foy, PQ G1X 3V6   Tel. (418) 658.3763
                                 Telefax: (418) 658.3763

Federal Publications Inc.
165 University Avenue, Suite 701
Toronto, ON M5H 3B8   Tel. (416) 860.1611
                                 Telefax: (416) 860.1608

Les Publications Fédérales
1185 Université
Montréal, QC H3B 3A7   Tel. (514) 954.1633
                                 Telefax: (514) 954.1635

CHINA – CHINE
China National Publications Import
Export Corporation (CNPIEC)
16 Gongti E. Road, Chaoyang District
P.O. Box 88 or 50
Beijing 100704 PR   Tel. (01) 506.6688
                                 Telefax: (01) 506.3101

CHINESE TAIPEI – TAIPEI CHINOIS
Good Faith Worldwide Int'l. Co. Ltd.
9th Floor, No. 118, Sec. 2
Chung Hsiao E. Road
Taipei   Tel. (02) 391.7396/391.7397
                                 Telefax: (02) 394.9176

CZECH REPUBLIC – RÉPUBLIQUE TCHÈQUE
Artia Pegas Press Ltd.
Narodni Trida 25
POB 825
111 21 Praha I   Tel. 26.65.68
                                 Telefax: 26.20.81

DENMARK – DANEMARK
Munksgaard Book and Subscription Service
35, Nørre Søgade, P.O. Box 2148
DK-1016 København K   Tel. (33) 12.85.70
                                 Telefax: (33) 12.93.87

EGYPT – ÉGYPTE
Middle East Observer
41 Sherif Street
Cairo   Tel. 392.6919
                                 Telefax: 360-6804

FINLAND – FINLANDE
Akateeminen Kirjakauppa
Keskuskatu 1, P.O. Box 128
00100 Helsinki
Subscription Services/Agence d'abonnements :
P.O. Box 23
00371 Helsinki   Tel. (358 0) 121 4416
                                 Telefax: (358 0) 121.4450

FRANCE
OECD/OCDE
Mail Orders/Commandes par correspondance:
2, rue André-Pascal
75775 Paris Cedex 16   Tel. (33-1) 45.24.82.00
                             Telefax: (33-1) 49.10.42.76
                             Telex: 640048 OCDE
Internet: Compte.PUBSINQ @ oecd.org
Orders via Minitel, France only/
Commandes par Minitel, France exclusivement :
36 15 OCDE

OECD Bookshop/Librairie de l'OCDE :
33, rue Octave-Feuillet
75016 Paris   Tel. (33-1) 45.24.81.81
                                 (33-1) 45.24.81.67
Documentation Française
29, quai Voltaire
75007 Paris   Tel. 40.15.70.00
Gibert Jeune (Droit-Économie)
6, place Saint-Michel
75006 Paris   Tel. 43.25.91.19
Librairie du Commerce International
10, avenue d'Iéna
75016 Paris   Tel. 40.73.34.60
Librairie Dunod
Université Paris-Dauphine
Place du Maréchal de Lattre de Tassigny
75016 Paris   Tel. (1) 44.05.40.13
Librairie Lavoisier
11, rue Lavoisier
75008 Paris   Tel. 42.65.39.95
Librairie L.G.D.J. - Montchrestien
20, rue Soufflot
75005 Paris   Tel. 46.33.89.85
Librairie des Sciences Politiques
30, rue Saint-Guillaume
75007 Paris   Tel. 45.48.36.02
P.U.F.
49, boulevard Saint-Michel
75005 Paris   Tel. 43.25.83.40
Librairie de l'Université
12a, rue Nazareth
13100 Aix-en-Provence   Tel. (16) 42.26.18.08
Documentation Française
165, rue Garibaldi
69003 Lyon   Tel. (16) 78.63.32.23
Librairie Decitre
29, place Bellecour
69002 Lyon   Tel. (16) 72.40.54.54
Librairie Sauramps
Le Triangle
34967 Montpellier Cedex 2   Tel. (16) 67.58.85.15
                             Tekefax: (16) 67.58.27.36

GERMANY – ALLEMAGNE
OECD Publications and Information Centre
August-Bebel-Allee 6
D-53175 Bonn   Tel. (0228) 959.120
                                 Telefax: (0228) 959.12.17

GREECE – GRÈCE
Librairie Kauffmann
Mavrokordatou 9
106 78 Athens   Tel. (01) 32.55.321
                                 Telefax: (01) 32.30.320

HONG-KONG
Swindon Book Co. Ltd.
Astoria Bldg. 3F
34 Ashley Road, Tsimshatsui
Kowloon, Hong Kong   Tel. 2376.2062
                                 Telefax: 2376.0685

HUNGARY – HONGRIE
Euro Info Service
Margitsziget, Európa Ház
1138 Budapest   Tel. (1) 111.62.16
                                 Telefax: (1) 111.60.61

ICELAND – ISLANDE
Mál Mog Menning
Laugavegi 18, Pósthólf 392
121 Reykjavik   Tel. (1) 552.4240
                                 Telefax: (1) 562.3523

INDIA – INDE
Oxford Book and Stationery Co.
Scindia House
New Delhi 110001   Tel. (11) 331.5896/5308
                                 Telefax: (11) 332.5993

17 Park Street
Calcutta 700016   Tel. 240832

INDONESIA – INDONÉSIE
Pdii-Lipi
P.O. Box 4298
Jakarta 12042   Tel. (21) 573.34.67
                                 Telefax: (21) 573.34.67

IRELAND – IRLANDE
Government Supplies Agency
Publications Section
4/5 Harcourt Road
Dublin 2   Tel. 661.31.11
                                 Telefax: 475.27.60

ISRAEL
Praedicta
5 Shatner Street
P.O. Box 34030
Jerusalem 91430   Tel. (2) 52.84.90/1/2
                                 Telefax: (2) 52.84.93

R.O.Y. International
P.O. Box 13056
Tel Aviv 61130   Tel. (3) 546 1423
                                 Telefax: (3) 546 1442

Palestinian Authority/Middle East:
INDEX Information Services
P.O.B. 19502
Jerusalem   Tel. (2) 27.12.19
                                 Telefax: (2) 27.16.34

ITALY – ITALIE
Libreria Commissionaria Sansoni
Via Duca di Calabria 1/1
50125 Firenze   Tel. (055) 64.54.15
                                 Telefax: (055) 64.12.57
Via Bartolini 29
20155 Milano   Tel. (02) 36.50.83
Editrice e Libreria Herder
Piazza Montecitorio 120
00186 Roma   Tel. 679.46.28
                                 Telefax: 678.47.51
Libreria Hoepli
Via Hoepli 5
20121 Milano   Tel. (02) 86.54.46
                                 Telefax: (02) 805.28.86
Libreria Scientifica
Dott. Lucio de Biasio 'Aeiou'
Via Coronelli, 6
20146 Milano   Tel. (02) 48.95.45.52
                                 Telefax: (02) 48.95.45.48

JAPAN – JAPON
OECD Publications and Information Centre
Landic Akasaka Building
2-3-4 Akasaka, Minato-ku
Tokyo 107   Tel. (81.3) 3586.2016
                                 Telefax: (81.3) 3584.7929

KOREA – CORÉE
Kyobo Book Centre Co. Ltd.
P.O. Box 1658, Kwang Hwa Moon
Seoul   Tel. 730.78.91
                                 Telefax: 735.00.30

MALAYSIA – MALAISIE
University of Malaya Bookshop
University of Malaya
P.O. Box 1127, Jalan Pantai Baru
59700 Kuala Lumpur
Malaysia   Tel. 756.5000/756.5425
                            Telefax: 756.3246

MEXICO – MEXIQUE
Revistas y Periodicos Internacionales S.A. de C.V.
Florencia 57 - 1004
Mexico, D.F. 06600   Tel. 207.81.00
                           Telefax: 208.39.79

NETHERLANDS – PAYS-BAS
SDU Uitgeverij Plantijnstraat
Externe Fondsen
Postbus 20014
2500 EA's-Gravenhage   Tel. (070) 37.89.880
Voor bestellingen: Telefax: (070) 34.75.778

**NEW ZEALAND
NOUVELLE-ZÉLANDE**
GPLegislation Services
P.O. Box 12418
Thorndon, Wellington   Tel. (04) 496.5655
                           Telefax: (04) 496.5698

NORWAY – NORVÈGE
Narvesen Info Center – NIC
Bertrand Narvesens vei 2
P.O. Box 6125 Etterstad
0602 Oslo 6   Tel. (022) 57.33.00
                          Telefax: (022) 68.19.01

PAKISTAN
Mirza Book Agency
65 Shahrah Quaid-E-Azam
Lahore 54000   Tel. (42) 353.601
                          Telefax: (42) 231.730

PHILIPPINE – PHILIPPINES
International Book Center
5th Floor, Filipinas Life Bldg.
Ayala Avenue
Metro Manila   Tel. 81.96.76
                        Telex 23312 RHP PH

PORTUGAL
Livraria Portugal
Rua do Carmo 70-74
Apart. 2681
1200 Lisboa   Tel. (01) 347.49.82/5
                          Telefax: (01) 347.02.64

SINGAPORE – SINGAPOUR
Gower Asia Pacific Pte Ltd.
Golden Wheel Building
41, Kallang Pudding Road, No. 04-03
Singapore 1334   Tel. 741.5166
                           Telefax: 742.9356

SPAIN – ESPAGNE
Mundi-Prensa Libros S.A.
Castelló 37, Apartado 1223
Madrid 28001   Tel. (91) 431.33.99
                          Telefax: (91) 575.39.98

Libreria Internacional AEDOS
Consejo de Ciento 391
08009 – Barcelona   Tel. (93) 488.30.09
                          Telefax: (93) 487.76.59

Llibreria de la Generalitat
Palau Moja
Rambla dels Estudis, 118
08002 – Barcelona
              (Subscripcions) Tel. (93) 318.80.12
              (Publicacions) Tel. (93) 302.67.23
                          Telefax: (93) 412.18.54

SRI LANKA
Centre for Policy Research
c/o Colombo Agencies Ltd.
No. 300-304, Galle Road
Colombo 3   Tel. (1) 574240, 573551-2
                  Telefax: (1) 575394, 510711

SWEDEN – SUÈDE
Fritzes Customer Service
S–106 47 Stockholm   Tel. (08) 690.90.90
                          Telefax: (08) 20.50.21

Subscription Agency/Agence d'abonnements :
Wennergren-Williams Info AB
P.O. Box 1305
171 25 Solna   Tel. (08) 705.97.50
                          Telefax: (08) 27.00.71

SWITZERLAND – SUISSE
Maditec S.A. (Books and Periodicals - Livres
et périodiques)
Chemin des Palettes 4
Case postale 266
1020 Renens VD 1   Tel. (021) 635.08.65
                          Telefax: (021) 635.07.80

Librairie Payot S.A.
4, place Pépinet
CP 3212
1002 Lausanne   Tel. (021) 341.33.47
                          Telefax: (021) 341.33.45

Librairie Unilivres
6, rue de Candolle
1205 Genève   Tel. (022) 320.26.23
                          Telefax: (022) 329.73.18

Subscription Agency/Agence d'abonnements :
Dynapresse Marketing S.A.
38 avenue Vibert
1227 Carouge   Tel. (022) 308.07.89
                          Telefax: (022) 308.07.99

See also – Voir aussi :
OECD Publications and Information Centre
August-Bebel-Allee 6
D-53175 Bonn (Germany)   Tel. (0228) 959.120
                          Telefax: (0228) 959.12.17

THAILAND – THAÏLANDE
Suksit Siam Co. Ltd.
113, 115 Fuang Nakhon Rd.
Opp. Wat Rajbopith
Bangkok 10200   Tel. (662) 225.9531/2
                          Telefax: (662) 222.5188

TURKEY – TURQUIE
Kültür Yayinlari Is-Türk Ltd. Sti.
Atatürk Bulvari No. 191/Kat 13
Kavaklidere/Ankara   Tel. 428.11.40 Ext. 2458
Dolmabahce Cad. No. 29
Besiktas/Istanbul   Tel. (312) 260 7188
                         Telex: (312) 418 29 46

UNITED KINGDOM – ROYAUME-UNI
HMSO
Gen. enquiries   Tel. (171) 873 8496
Postal orders only:
P.O. Box 276, London SW8 5DT
Personal Callers HMSO Bookshop
49 High Holborn, London WC1V 6HB
                           Telefax: (171) 873 8416
Branches at: Belfast, Birmingham, Bristol,
Edinburgh, Manchester

UNITED STATES – ÉTATS-UNIS
OECD Publications and Information Center
2001 L Street N.W., Suite 650
Washington, D.C. 20036-4910 Tel. (202) 785.6323
                          Telefax: (202) 785.0350

VENEZUELA
Libreria del Este
Avda F. Miranda 52, Aptdo. 60337
Edificio Galipán
Caracas 106   Tel. 951.1705/951.2307/951.1297
                    Telegram: Libreste Caracas

Subscription to OECD periodicals may also be
placed through main subscription agencies.

Les abonnements aux publications périodiques de
l'OCDE peuvent être souscrits auprès des
principales agences d'abonnement.

Orders and inquiries from countries where Distribu-
tors have not yet been appointed should be sent to:
OECD Publications Service, 2 rue André-Pascal,
75775 Paris Cedex 16, France.

Les commandes provenant de pays où l'OCDE n'a
pas encore désigné de distributeur peuvent être
adressées à : OCDE, Service des Publications,
2, rue André-Pascal, 75775 Paris Cedex 16, France.

7-1995

OECD PUBLICATIONS, 2 rue André-Pascal, 75775 PARIS CEDEX 16
PRINTED IN FRANCE
(21 95 12 1) ISBN 92-64-14635-0 - No. 48283 1995